PASSPORT TO FREEDOM

Education, Humanism, and Malcolm X

PASSPORT

TO   FREEDOM

EDUCATION,

HUMANISM,

& MALCOLM X

by Charles G. Hurst, Jr.

1972
LINNET BOOKS · HAMDEN · CONNECTICUT

Library of Congress Cataloging in Publication Data
Hurst, Charles G.
   Passport to freedom.
   Bibliography: p. 225–234
   1. Negroes—Education.   2. Malcolm X College.
I. Title.
LC2801.H8   371.9'67   73–146656
ISBN 0–208–01200–1

Published as a Linnet Book by
The Shoe String Press, Inc.
Hamden, Connecticut, USA

Printed in the United States of America

This book is dedicated to all my children whom
I love very much. I pray it will serve to encourage
them in their own efforts to free this world
of hate, injustice, and inhumanity.

CONTENTS

A Message
from
Betty Shabazz

My husband, Malcolm X El Hadjj El Malik Shabazz, spent much of his extraordinary life articulating the despair of Black people. He inspired millions to seek new horizons of humanistic achievement but he put his hope in the young. And now there is a reverence and an excitement about his memory that holds special meanings for Black youth.

He is still sorely missed and greatly loved by his six children and me, and by Black people everywhere.

Malcolm's birthday is Wednesday, May 19, and the dedication of the new campus of Chicago's Malcolm X College was held on that day in 1971.

The College, devoted and dedicated to Black excellence in education and in all other human endeavor, is a great tribute to his memory. This book is a further tribute to his belief in the ultimate integrity of humanity.

The book is not, however, only a tribute to my husband, Malcolm. It is the embodiment of his philosophy, a philosophy of life forged from his experiences and a philosophy of education as reflected by his many statements in this field. It represents also the philosophy of a movement, begun perhaps by my husband, toward a more humanistic approach to the development of human potential.

In my view, this book is written for all people who are interested in promoting the well-being of all other people. It is about education, but it is not exclusively for educators, neither does it seek to exclude them. It is about the plight of Black people, but it does not pretend to be all inclusive or even authoritative on this subject. It presents the plight of Black people, desperate as it is in the U.S.A., more as a barometer of existing conditions in dire need of attention throughout the world if mankind is to ever have peace as a way of life.

Explicit in these chapters is the nature of the times in which we live and the experiences that Black people continue to endure in our struggle for full freedom from the slavery imposed upon us over a period exceeding four hundred years. Much has been written about education and its faults, but little from the Black point of view. *Passport to Freedom* describes and probes the social dilemmas affecting the lives of Black people and threatening their survival. It outlines the types of educational reforms needed to revolutionize their existence, and cites some processes required for a better humanity throughout the world and for the kind of domestic tranquility for which we should all aspire.

The book is simply the reflections of one Black man on conditions as they now exist; crying out with another voice for the justice long denied the minorities of this country. Yet he does not pretend to have all the answers for the complex problems that are part of life in the seventies.

The book calls for educational change, in a way that should not alienate scholars, but in a way that will appeal to those clamoring for revolutionary change and relevance. Underscored throughout the criticisms of education that occur in the book is the belief that the past cannot be totally discarded as efforts are made toward a more hopeful future.

The author also supports the notion that massive change is required in the moral basis for our existence as people as well as in education. Most pleasing to me is the way he has stressed a kind of basic humanity that is often missing in today's world. He describes a humanity that is built on such moral qualities as courage, faith, determination, perseverance, and loyalty to a worthy cause. Decency, ingenuity, and sensitivity are also implicit in the hierarchy of values upon which the author would build universal concepts of freedom and human rights.

And finally, the book talks without condescension of an approach to education for the Black urban masses that could become the prototype needed so urgently to cope with prevailing frustrations. The experiences of Malcolm X College, not spelled out in detail, are put forth as simply one set of examples of how creative efforts by competent persons can generate a vastly improved environment for developing human potential.

It is important, however, that the underlying plea which may really be the book's central theme not go unheeded. Injustice, whether in education or elsewhere, must be relegated to the ignoble past. Any future we may hope to have may well depend on it.

BETTY SHABAZZ

FOREWORD

The African Heritage

These remarks were given originally as a speech by the author on May 19, 1971 at the dedication of the new Malcolm X College campus in Chicago. It seemed fitting that these words should become the foreword to the book, Passport to Freedom.

This is a great day in the history of Black America! The flag of the Black nation has been raised over a public building in the U. S. A. for the first time in all of our history. The symbolic significance of this flag will have far-reaching effects from this day forward. Its connection with the past should also be quite clear. Brother Lou Palmer tells us:

> The top red is for the blood all Black people have shed and must continue to shed in order to achieve the Black Nation.
>
> The second bar is black, representing our race. Our civilization predates all others and although we have fallen on evil days, we will rise again to take our rightful place in the world.
>
> The third bar is green, symbolic of land and nationhood. No people can be truly free unless they have a land base. Land is the basis of power and freedom. The Black flag means Black nationalism and Black nationalism means land and power.

I thank the many people who made this day possible by helping create Malcolm X College. They are too numerous to name,
but they are all around me: the chancellor, the chairman of the
Board, vice-presidents, deans, directors, teachers, and just plain
folks.

It has taken all kinds of people. But that's the important
thing about our College, the people who are building it. Together
we are building an institution of power. More important, we are
building an organization of people to meet the needs of today,
and we are building the people who will be the leaders of
tomorrow.

I am deeply proud of what we are doing. Not because of the
brick, mortar, steel, and glass that constitute our beautiful new
campus, but because of what we achieved in the old one. This
institution made its mark while we were located in the dilapidated quarters that are now a part of our past.

The greatness of our institution now as then is in the people.
It is in understanding the importance of people that we shall
achieve the power needed to forge education into an instrument
of self-liberation. The significance of this goal should not be un-
derestimated. As Ellis Cose, the fine young Black columnist with
the Chicago Sun–Times, has said, "The man who controls education controls the mind. The man who controls the mind can
control the world."

Black people are on the way to somewhere. You had better
believe it! And if you don't know where Blacks are heading,
keep on listening.

May 19th is Malcolm's birthday—a day that has become a
precious part of our heritage. It is precious because of what Malcolm left us as his greatest contribution to mankind—an almost
indescribably beautiful, wondrous humanism. Malcolm's was the
kind of humanism that America must develop on a broad scale
if it is to survive as a nation. It must have in unprecedented
abundance a new type of man and woman dedicated to humanism and love of humanity as a way of life.

If anyone asks me, What are we about at Malcolm X College?
If they ask: Are you developing doctors? Are you developing en-

gineers? Are you developing teachers? Are you developing social workers? I would answer to them: Yes! All of these. But we are doing something much more important and much greater. We are developing dedicated, honest, informed humanists who will be the leadership of tomorrow.

We are developing a kind of leader who submerges himself in service to the community. The kind of leader who recognizes that there is no way under this glorious sun that one Black man can be free until every other living Black man in the entire world is free. We are developing the kind of leader whose ability to love is his strength and whose integrity is his greatness.

Ours is a new approach to achieving the goals of education. We proceed in the belief that you cannot deprive young people of the right of social responsibility, social consciousness, and the ability to judge social issues while they are in school, and then expect them to become experts at these when they leave school. It is not probable.

One of the most important factors in education ought to be the opportunity to be engaged in *doing* something meaningful at the same time as the mind is being honed to a fine intellectual edge. There also should be a strong underlying social motive in the business of education to assure an effective learning situation. Moreover, the student must be made aware that what he is doing, what he is learning, will help him eventually to improve the nature of his own condition and contribute substantially to the good of the entire society. What he is to learn in school must hold the promise for him that it will someday help him to liberate himself and his people. If his experiences as a student do not deal with the liberation of himself and his people, it becomes for him an irrelevant education and is most often considered by him as not worth getting in the first place.

What I am stressing today, however, is that what we have achieved during the past few years has brought us to the verge of a moment of greatness; a precious moment that doesn't occur often in the course of human history.

At the moment of man's first presence on the moon it was said that a great first step had been taken. Reminiscence does not dim the courage of the men who achieved that feat or the almost miraculous skill of the technicians who made it possible. The achievement was a monument to what man can do when man develops a deep and irrevocable sense of commitment. But this was not a moment of true greatness, only a technological miracle. It did nothing to assure that there will be no more poverty, that there will be no more hunger, that there will be no more injustice, that there will be no more hate, that there will be no more Angela Davises who will have to suffer in jail when they have done nothing wrong. I wonder if we will *ever* be able to will these things as we willed that we should go to the moon. It will be a truly great moment for all of us when these conditions are made a permanent part of the past.

A lofty aspiration? All our aspirations for mankind are lofty, because we seek to guarantee that one day man will achieve the potential of his greatness in human areas as he has achieved so astoundingly in technical areas.

I hope these words are making quite clear what Malcolm X College has come to mean to me, and the basic truths upon which the philosophy of our College has been built.

And it is rather natural to me that new basic truths, new insights for education in America, and a revised system of values should be formulated by African people. It is not inconsistent that education in America should be redefining itself—through such colleges as Malcolm X—to include the richness and the creativity of America's African heritage which it has ignored for so long.

The tragedies of recent history should have taught all of us that the values so inherent in the heritage of African people must no longer be sacrificed unheedingly in the pursuit of material progress. We can no longer permit ourselves to become consumed by a desire for material things—big cars and fine clothes and all of that—when all around us there is so much suffering. We must remember always while we seek economic advancement for our people that we must work hand in hand to raise the standard of life for all people.

In essence, we must never become willing to sacrifice the fundamental humanity that is part of the African genius. We need this to redirect America in its search for greatness.

When I speak of the African genius, I am not only speaking of Negritude, nor do I speak solely of a brotherhood based on color. The African genius that I speak of is our concept of a great society based on a highly developed code of morals, purposeful energy expended for the collective good, and a great sense of humanitarianism. The African genius is, then, defined most effectively by the cluster of humanistic principles which underlie the traditional African society.

It is very important that all in America understand as Black people proceed in our quest for a revival of our culture that if the country is to survive it must develop strong moral and spiritual foundations and we can help it to do just that.

It is the immorality that has been allowed to accrue in this nation that is taking it down the present path threatening destruction. Only a lack of sincere moral convictions could have persuaded this nation to go all over the world trying to solve other nation's problems without solving the problems right here at home.

The price has been so high. I don't know if you are aware of how many people have died already in Vietnam—more than 54,000. Another 250,000 or more have been wounded, many crippled for life.

A disproportionate number of all those killed and maimed were young Black men fighting abroad to gain freedom for somebody else when they did not enjoy that same right in their own country.

But, in spite of the continued pressure of an environment filled with violence and decaying morals, our own spiritual and moral qualities must not lag behind the progress that we hope to make in areas of economic, social and political endeavor. Further, they must be no less lofty than our aspirations in all areas.

And what are our aspirations as a people?

Our basic concern is with the right of all people to decide their own destiny and to make their own way through life in freedom. We view freedom as an inalienable right of all people that must not be encumbered in any way, so long as the expression of that right does not interfere with other rights basic to human existence. Freedom as we view it is so fundamental to remaining human that it must someday be ours, even if we have to take it by whatever means are at our disposal.

But it follows that if we really desire freedom so desperately and believe in truth that it is really our right, we must be willing, not to ask for it nor to beg for it, but to demand it and to fight for it. Eventually, we ourselves must become able to direct the institutions in our community that shape and control the lives of our people. Only in this way can we guarantee our own survival and contribute to that of Black people everywhere.

Our aims beyond this, however, are for all in this country. This is the way of African people. We would like to make the United States a worthy place to live for all of its citizens. We would like to prove that greatness is not measured by stockpiles of nuclear weapons.

As African people, we believe and would like others to believe strongly and sincerely in the deep rooted dignity of the human spirit and the respect it deserves. We would like to see also a universal respect for human life and the abolishment of violence as a way of settling differences.

The intense humanity that is the heritage of African people can help this country emerge as a truly great power, based on a new concern for all human beings rather than on a platform of fear, envy, suspicion, and hate.

We have begun this great task that is ours right here at Malcolm X College. We are extending our task by promising to everybody within earshot and farther to make our college a shining light throughout the city of Chicago, giving inspiration far beyond its corporate limits. And this we can do! We can do it by dedicating ourselves, each of us, individually and collectively, through unselfish service to creating a better world for all people. We can do it by moving ahead side by side with other warriors of dedication, armed with knowledge, armed with ideas, armed with determination, armed with courage, and armed with our humanity.

We will measure our progress by the improvements in the life conditions of our people, by the number of our young people who are again in school because school has become relevant to them, by the quality of the education that they are getting, and by the happiness that comes from managing our own lives.

But if we are to achieve these important goals, we as a people must have a unity of spirit and purpose, as well as dedication. These are among the most important of the preconditions for ultimate success. The kind of unity I speak of requires that every single person become aware of who he is, what must be done, and the role he must play in the struggle for freedom.

Each of us must also come to know what Black awareness means in terms of ourselves. It should not be construed as simply learning about our past but learning what we will need to control our own destinies and learning that it is about time we develop the determination to build our own nation. Both of these, together with mutual respect, are inevitable if we are ever to liberate ourselves.

There is no doubt also that we must develop the kind of determination exemplified by Malcolm X and Martin Luther King. That is the only kind of determination that can guarantee our ultimate victory over bigotry and injustice.

But as we pursue our goals there are certain precepts that we must always live by and there can be no deviation from these. Basic among them are seven principles that I would commend to you. Every one should be memorized and considered each and every day.

UMOJA	*Unity*: to strive for and maintain unity in the family, in the community, in our nation and throughout our race.
KUJICHAGULIA	*Self-determination*: to define ourselves, to name ourselves and to speak for ourselves, instead of being defined, and spoken for by somebody else all the time.
UJIMA	*Collective work and collective responsibility*: to build and to maintain our

community together, and to make our brothers' and sisters' problems our problems, and to solve them together.

UJAMAA

Co-operative economics: to build and maintain our institutions, our own store, and shops, and to profit together from them, swearing that we will never live by exploitation of each other.

NIA

Purpose: to make as our collective vocation the building and developing of our community in order to restore our people to their traditional greatness.

KUUMBA

Creativity: to do always as much as we can, in the way that we can, in order to leave our community more beautiful and beneficial than when we inherited it.

IMANI

Faith: the faith without which no people can survive. The faith to believe with all our hearts in our parents, in our teachers, in our leaders, in our people, in ourselves, in the righteousness of our struggle, and in the ultimate victory that will be ours.

The unity and eventual liberation of Black people will grow out of unswerving adherence to these kinds of principles. We must come to understand this.

Again, I say to you that out of the spirit of this College is coming a renewal of the manhood that Malcolm X stood for. We are producing as a result a kind of man who is afraid of nothing and nobody; a man who knows that the love of his people is the greatest honor any man can hope to achieve. To be able to serve his people ought to be the end product of every man's life.

Because of what we are doing, I see a future leadership that will give the country the hope it has been seeking for so long. A leadership for every aspect of life—a leadership in medicine; a leadership in law; a leadership in justice; a leadership in urban affairs; a leadership in all aspects of the nation's existence. All be-

because at such places as Malcolm X College we are dedicating ourselves to creating a society in which men, women, and children will no longer have anxiety about food, shelter, respect, and freedom. Because we have committed ourselves to building a society where poverty and illiteracy no longer exist—where disease has been brought under control, where our educational facilities provide our children with the best possible opportunities for learning, where every person uses his talents to their fullest capacity and contributes to the general well-being of his nation steadily and consistently—the future outlook is not as bleak as it has been.

And as we proceed, we shall be building step by step the road to a better and richer life for all people, developing a society free from racial discrimination, developing a society in which people of different beliefs can work together without molestation or fear, a society in which the relations between men shall be based only on noble truths rather than on such irrelevancies as social status and power. All this we believe we can do.

And in our school, we have no place for the nonbelievers, just as we have no place for those who cannot see faith and morality as important cornerstones of our existence. We have no place for shirkers. We have places only for the thinkers and the doers, because ours is a concept of self-help, efficiency, enterprise, excellence, and achievement. Our school is an institution born out of the suffering and the courage of many heroes, Malcolm X one—probably the greatest. It is a place of opportunity for active minds and dedicated people.

We know that we carry a heavy responsibility. We also know that no one of us need bear that responsibility alone.

What I see before each and every one of us is a noble and a glorious challenge—a challenge that calls for a kind of person that we have not had ordinarily: a dreamer with the guts to make his dream a challenge; a challenge that calls for the courage to dream greater dreams; a challenge that calls for the courage to believe; a challenge that calls for the courage to dare; a challenge that calls for the courage to do, the courage to envision, the courage to fight when necessary, the courage to work, the courage to achieve—to achieve the highest excellence on God's earth and the fullness and the greatness of which man is so capable.

Dare any one of us ask for more in this life than to give to our people all of the essence of ourselves, and to help our people strive for the excellence of which they are capable? Is there anything greater in life, I would ask you, than contributing to the welfare of mankind through a life of service?

I must say finally that if you do not pledge yourself to the kinds of goals outlined here, if you do not understand the message of our beautiful flag, if you cannot understand the need of the community for your service, and if you cannot understand the role that you must play in every waking moment of your life until the struggle for liberation is won, then there is a long road ahead for you and not much hope for me or you. Each and every one of us must achieve self-awareness and a realization of what must be done if the future is to be made secure.

I am so impressed by the greatness of our potential that there is no way words can fully express what I feel. The future of this country may well *become* secure because of the creative genius of people who never ceased their quest for freedom and never lost their humanity while doing so.

We must now go about the business of completing our work.

May God bless each and every one of you, and I thank you so much for joining us in this tribute to our new beginnings.

ACKNOWLEDGMENTS

I am sincerely grateful for the assistance given me in completing this work by Mrs. Davie McGill and Mrs. Shirley Knazze. A very special thanks is due my wife Beverly whose patience was indispensable to completing the task. I thank also the students of Malcolm X College, the Black community of the city of Chicago, and the many fine people who were willing to listen and comment upon the ideas that are the basis for this book. Finally, I thank the Chicago *Tribune* which first printed the material on Black literature and "Malcolm X the Man," and the Chicago *Daily News* which first printed the review of A *Rap on Race*.

C.G.H., Jr.

> *. . . a book is both written and read, and even if it is not read very accurately, its message, to a point, is what the reader makes of it.*
>
> David Caute

INTRODUCTION

Too much of what we do in social affairs is uncalculated as compared with the great care taken in preparing for confrontation or innovation involving physical phenomena. Human events are permitted to just happen. After they happen we react. Education is a principal victim of this tendency.

In a meeting convened by the National Council of Churches, Congressman William Ford stated:

> We simply do not have a national commitment to education. Nobody in the history of this country has been defeated or even harmed in any way by his outright opposition to or phony support of federal aid to education. We get what we want most from our government.
>
> If we had devoted in this country the same kind of resources and the same percentage of our wealth and the same commitment in the aircraft industries as we have in education, John Glenn would still be sitting out in the field someplace trying to get off the ground in a gas-filled balloon.

This statement accentuates in a rather stark manner the nature of the tragic mistakes made by the nation's leaders with

respect to education in a twentieth-century society. Its format
and techniques have changed little since the nineteenth century
for which it was designed. But this is not the only problem of
our educational system confronting us now.

Paulo Freire, education director for the World Council of
Churches, remarked at the same meeting called by the NCC
about what is increasingly becoming a central concern for con-
scientious educators, the unwillingness to view education as an
instrument for bringing about change.

> It is important to emphasize the impossibility of neutral edu-
> cation. It is either for liberation or domestication. Education
> either functions as an instrument to integrate the younger gen-
> eration into the logic of the present system and bring about con-
> formity to it, or education becomes the means by which men
> and women deal critically and creatively with reality and dis-
> cover how to participate in the transformation of their world.
> Most often we think we are working for the liberation and hu-
> manization of men but by the methods we use we prevent men
> from becoming free.

This statement emphasizes the second most important failure
involving education: our neglect of education as a weapon to
fight bigotry, support humanism, build great ideas, and promote
the full liberation of all people.

Perhaps the greatest tragedy of our time grows out of the in-
excusable ignorance throughout white America about citizens
of African origin. Few white Americans, whether school dropouts or college graduates, know more than a smattering about
the Black American's contribution to this nation's history, culture, and survival. Most of what they do know is myth, some of
it harmless but much of it viciously demeaning and designed to
create false impressions of white superiority and Black inferiority.
Until this disgraceful set of conditions is eliminated a genuine
basis for mutual respect can never exist, and the festering anger
of impatient Black Americans will continue to mount.

It is still incredible that so many of the "educated" white people in the United States believe that large numbers of Black
people are shiftless, destructive, happy-go-lucky, and mentally inferior. Yet it is not so surprising when one reviews the intensity

with which the general public has been conditioned to accept these myths. Movies, radio, television, books, and particularly the schools have combined to perpetuate an Amos and Andy or a Stepin Fechit image for the Black male. The practice has been so systematic and all pervasive that the Black man came for a time to believe many of the myths about himself.

Although the "good old mammy" image for the Black female was degrading the treatment of the Black male was and continues to be vicious, tearing at his manhood in every possible way, stripping him of his dignity, and creating a self-hate possessed with deadly potential. As the Black psychologist Charles Thomas in a speech delivered June 8, 1968 puts it: ". . . education has crippled more of us than all of the diseases of mankind."

So thorough were the effects of the brainwashing on the Black Americans, that we spent amazing sums attempting to lose our identity. We were taught to view Africa as a continent of primitive people surviving only because of the missionary benevolence of white colonialists. We were taught also to be ashamed of our own physical characteristics. Our concept of beauty was based on a white model of western European origin. So, not surprisingly in the face of a persisting desire to be accepted as equals, bleaching creams to make the skin lighter and various methods of making the hair straighter became major sale items in the Black community. It was a pitiful situation to see poor people without enough to meet minimum dietary needs spending hard-earned dollars on cosmetics in an effort to redesign their identity and make it more acceptable to their white tormentors.

Wesley T. Cobb, Associate director, National Urban League, points out:

> To see more of the consequences of cultural stripping, ask yourself a few questions. How many American-born Negroes do you know, whose names are Kenyatta, Luthuli, or Mboya? These are African names. Names like these were lost through cultural stripping of slaves who were the African ancestors of the Negro in America. How many Negroes, born in America, do you know whose religion is not one of the dominant patterns of religion in this country? The "Black Muslims" are an exception, but this is in fact an innovation, a cultural product of twentieth-century

America. How many Negroes, American born, do you know who speak Swahili, Yoruba, Sudanese, or Bantu? These are among the many languages of the American Negro's African ancestors.

In the early 1950s the emergence of the Rev. Dr. Martin Luther King Jr., as a dedicated fighter for the cause of civil and human rights for all, introduced a new era of awareness for Black people. Himself the picture of stern dignity, King became the prototype for a new model of Black male courage. His use of the boycott, militant marches, angry rhetoric, and civil disobedience as weapons of liberation made Black people all over the country aware that the period of passive acquiescence to injustice was over. The Black man became imbued with a new belief: *I Am Somebody*. He became obsessed with the idea that freedom is not only his right under God and the United States Constitution, but a necessity if he is going to avoid obliteration as a human being.

The Civil Rights Movement, as most call it, succeeded in spotlighting the problems of Black America. But the response generated by murders of three young civil rights workers in Mississippi, the bombing of a church in Alabama, the use of dogs and cattle prods in Birmingham, and the callous brutality evidenced in Selma, soon settled into a renewed lethargy.

What was defined as tokenism by many in the Black community became movement that was "too fast" for many in the white community. A white backlash, as irrational as much else in the syndrome of racial discrimination, paved the way for the new demagogic bigotry of George Wallace and that of the neo-Nazi party.

Somehow a peculiar kind of pseudopatriotism became intertwined with the reaction of whites to Black protest. In North Carolina, billboards appeared with the statement: "This is klan country. Love it or leave it." In other parts of America sanctimonious whites tired of being reminded of their individual and collective guilt, but unwilling to support corrective action at the required level, leaped upon this new device for silencing criticism through making protest unpatriotic. "America, love it or leave it" became a new catch phrase.

Black youth, viewing the lack of real results for Black people as a whole, became angrily disillusioned with the nonviolent approach of Dr. King. They began to look cynically on the idea of an interracial brotherhood as the vehicle for resolving their grievances.

When the cry *Black Power!* burst from the lips of Stokely Carmichael during a speech given in the countryside of Mississippi it signalled the beginning of still another era, one to be marked by fury, violence, and rebellion. This era is still with us, reforming itself from time to time, but crystallizing as a permanent mood until true freedom is won.

Much of the tone for the new state of things was set by Malcolm X, the Muslim minister, whose early life was marked by the kind of persecution and suffering that is so typical for Black youth everywhere in America. Out of his speeches came a new theory of liberation, a new concept of Blackness, a new outlook on human rights.

Malcolm's grassroots level of understanding revealing the unique dilemma of Black people in America was underscored in the following statements he made in a conversation with Wesley T. Cobb:

> When you meet and talk with these good people, black or white, say to them that I am a Negro who signifies a new breed. I am a black man not born in the South. Although I am a product of the South's history, I did not come out of Mississippi or Alabama or Georgia. I came out of Michigan and Illinois. Say to these people—these good people—that I was a nappy-headed nigger who smelled bad, who talked bad, and acted bad, who had bad grades in school. But despite all of this badness I knew that I had some ability. I told myself that, and because I could tell myself that, I reached out for some help.
>
> I reached out to the good people in every town I lived in for some help. They said no. They couldn't see past my nappy head. They couldn't see past my raggedy clothes. They couldn't see me for looking and smelling and running.
>
> The people who helped me were the wrong people, from the point of view of the moral society, from the point of view of the democratic society. The people who helped me, whose hands reached out to mine, whose hearts and heads touched mine, were

the pimps, the prostitutes and hustlers, the thieves, and the mur-
derers. The people who helped me through the high school of
adolescence were the kids up in the reformatory. The people who
helped me through the college of life were the people up in the
prisons. And the people who helped me to get graduate training
in the university of common sense were the people out on the
streets, in the ghettos that were infested with crime and delinquency.

Say this to them, because man there are a whole lot of kids on
this street just like me. They smell bad, they act bad, they talk
bad, and their report card says they're dumb. But you know
something? These kids are smart. These kids are beautiful. These
kids are great. They need to be seen and helped.

The introduction of Black Studies is more than a rewriting
of history to include the Black American. It is a recognition that
a total reorganization of knowledge and curriculum must occur
if intellectual honesty is again to be a characteristic of our educational system. Included among its aims is the sociopsychologi-
cal rehabilitation of Africans in America, a goal that colleges had
previously not considered and were not prepared to set. Consequently when the early waves of students recruited by schools
attempting to meet "quotas" hit the campuses, they encountered
a familiar setting. The "white" college campus resembled for
them what Bartley Mc Swine called in *Change* magazine (May-
June, 1971) ". . . a white plantation; an existentialist island of
despair and hopelessness. . . . The air hangs heavy with pedagogy, but it is white pedagogy, with white roles and white rewards."

Referring to the mask that Paul Laurence Dunbar first alluded
to that many Black people wear in the presence of whites,
Mc Swine uses the words of Charles Gordone, the playwright, to
dramatize what being Black is all about. The words dramatize
better than most others the dimension of life in America that
the majority of white Americans know little about:

> They's mo' to bein' black than meets the eye!
> Bein' black, is like the way ya walk an' talk!
> It's a way'a lookin' at life!
> Bein' black, is like sayin', "Wha's happenin',

Babeee! An' bein' understood!
Bein' black has a way'a makin' ya call some-
Body a mu-tha-fuc-kah, an' really meanin' it!
An' namin' eva'body broh-thah, even if you don't!
Bein' black, is eatin' chit-lins an' wah-tah-
Melon, an' to hell with anybody, if they don't
like it!
Bein' black has a way'a makin' ya wear bright
Colors an' knowin' what a fine hat or a good
Pair'a shoes look like. . . .
It has a way'a makin' ya fingerpop! Invent a
New dance! Sing the blues! Drink good Scotch!
Smoke a big seegar while pushing a black Cadillac
With white sidewall tires! (It's wearin' an Afro-
Hairdo.) It's conkin' yo' head! Wearin' a black
Rag to keep the wave! Carryin' a razor.
(Readin' Richard Wright and Leroi Jones!)
Smokin' boo an' listenin' to gut-bucket jazz!
Yes! They's mo to bein' black than meets the eye!
—It's all the stuff that nobody wants but cain't
Live without! It's the body that keeps us standin'!
The soul that keeps us goin'! An' the spirit that'll
Take us thooo!
Yes; They's mo' to bein' black than meets the
eye!

[From *Chicago Magazine*, May/June, 1971.]

The main hope for education as a whole lies in a renewed willingness to admit that it is not enough to try doing the same thing better. A means must be found to break the existing monopoly of old institutions on available funds and legitimize the Nairobi Colleges, the street academies, and other alternative institutions. Without innovation from inside and outside of the present system we face no other choice then to go on struggling with the antiquated models provided by Harvards and other antiquated schools based on the past rather than the future.

Admittedly change is not easily induced.

Innovation was much talked about during the sixties with little actual change resulting in the way things were done in the classroom. In addition to the usual reticence of educators, the advent of unionism and the lack of a practical training for teachers combined to abort the creative efforts attempted sporadically in various parts of the country.

Very frequently new approaches were introduced with considerable fanfare. Team teaching and ungraded classrooms were sabotaged intentionally and unintentionally by teachers who felt far more comfortable with their structured, private-domain classrooms, and with a method of grading that threatened only the student, not the teacher's role as an all-knowing authoritarian.

In the seventies the money pinch has combined with demands for better education for all people to awaken new interest in utilizing contemporary technology and revitalized methods for developing intellectual potential. It is certainly about time. As the only way of meeting our responsibility for educating the masses, technology must be viewed as an asset rather than being referred to caustically as the bane of the technocrats. The approach recommended would follow in large measure the basic principles of cybernetics theory so that computers, auto-tutorial systems, and information retrieval systems would be placed at the service of humanity.

This is most important in the light of new understandings concerning learning, learning styles, and the interpretations placed on each. We are coming to know, for example, that there are many styles of learning. Different individuals learn in different ways without loss of efficiency with respect to outcomes. Although it may take one person longer than another to achieve a certain competence, there may be no relationship between the time taken to learn and the quality of the finished products. We know now that several of our most famous presidents would never have made the grade if school performance had been an important criterion.

Essentially, the "slower" learner may make a much greater social contribution. In any event, concepts of educational elitism and top ten percents are totally invalid because methods of measuring educational potential and educational outcomes are still at the stone-age level.

One area of urgent need has been attacked with some success.

This one outside the classroom but irrevocably interrelated to what happens inside.

In August of 1971 the Supreme Court of the State of California struck down local property tax as an equitable means of financing public school education. Basically, the court ruled that California's system of funding public schools primarily from local property taxes is unconstitutional because it denies children and taxpayers in poor school districts the "equal protection of the laws." The court noted that some school districts are rich in taxable property and can raise large sums to educate their children without taxing themselves heavily, while other districts are so poor that not even high tax rates can produce enough money to provide a good education. Since education is a "fundamental interest" of the state, the court held, its quality cannot be allowed to vary on the basis of the relative wealth of different districts, even if the state closes part of the financial gap with "equalization aid."

The Court also noted that the system of school financing dependent upon the community's own affluence resulted in pupil expenditure discrepancies of as much as $2,000 per child between high income and low-income school districts. The Court expressed the belief that the effectiveness of the educational programs varied as greatly when measured by the usual indices: graduates, dropouts, college-bound and admitted to college, equipment required for up-to-date science instruction, experienced teachers, physical facilities, books, learning aids, teacher and staff attitudes, and a host of other factors related to appropriate student motivation and achievement.

It was Arthur E. Wise, now associate dean of the Graduate School of Education at the University of Chicago, who first advocated applying the equal protection clause to public school finance. The argument advanced in his 1967 dissertation on the subject has been used as the basis of lawsuits in more than a dozen states, including Illinois.

Philip Kurland, a noted constitutional authority at the University of Chicago, also has stressed the belief that: "What we need is equality of output, which involves distributing resources so that all students can achieve at a given level. That, of course, will involve higher expenditures in some districts than others," but on a basis the reverse of present practice.

The action by the California court was a milestone for a variety of reasons. The turmoil accompanying the opening of schools all over the country in September of 1971 bore ample witness to the existence of an unprecedented level of frustration for all concerned with education. Taxpayers, whether parents or not, were expressing concern over the growing inability of schools to achieve consistent results on a broad scale, in the low-income areas of large, medium-size, and even small cities. Business and industrial spokesmen decried the quality of programs purporting to teach skills that were found to be inferior when students applied for employment. School administrators cried long and hard because of their inability to balance budgets stretched into grotesque shape through salary gains won by the insatiable demands of militant teacher's unions. Where accord was not reached, teachers in countless districts simply refused to permit schools to open.

The Board of Education in Chicago responded to the money crisis by decreeing a 12-day shutdown of the schools in December, an action which nullified all of the salary gains won during the previous school year by the Teachers' Union. In Philadelphia, the Board reduced costs by eliminating the last twelve days of the academic year. Both actions solved the fiscal crises temporarily but only postponed the more important crisis growing out of failure to meet adequately the educational needs of millions of aspiring people.

Chief among those victimized by the inability of the educational system to stabilize itself, for whatever reason, are the Chicano, Indian, Puerto Rican, Asian and Black people who have been discriminated against on a variety of other counts for an interminable period. Most prominent among these victimized minorities are the Black masses of America's cities, deltas, and rural enclaves. Yet the dilemma is the same for all. As a result, when analyzing as we attempt in this book the underlying problems of American education in relation to Black Americans, one is actually studying the full range of social issues as they relate to all Americans.

The failure of Newark's ghetto schools, for example, was cited by a Governor's Commission on Civil Disorders as a major cause of unrest as typified by the 1967 rebellions by Black youth in Newark. Of the 88 school buildings in Newark, four are more than 100 years old. Twenty-five are more than 50 years old. Many now being used were condemned in 1942. The worst of these were in the area where civil explosions took place.

So recommendations for change that are applicable to schools in the Black community are with few exceptions as relevant for any other community. Yet there *is* a need for a specific examination of the current state of education for Black people, factors contributing to unsatisfactory conditions, promising trends, and reforms that are essential for improved results. It seems important also to share with those interested some of the prevailing thought in the Black community on matters of general concern and to reveal certain important attitudes that affect in a profound way the status of race relations and domestic peace throughout the country. That's what this book is all about.

If the book meets its charge, a few more people may be enlightened about conditions and attitudes that are a part of life in the seventies. The book does not pretend to offer any panacea. It does attempt through examining the profusion of despair comprising life for neglected minorities, to introduce a valid optimism. Nothing new is presented for the sophisticated witness to today's events. The collection of subjects addressed does, however, represent a vitally important concentration of concerns with which all sincere people should be reasonably familiar. The dilemma of education, the tragedy of being Black, and the effects of racism for all of us are presented in prelude to discussions of educational revolutions through Black studies curricula, books on the Black experience, and new outlooks on some key issues involving human potential, learning styles, and educational goals.

Malcolm X, the college and the man, are included in the book more as examples of new trends, new alternatives, new strategies, and new determinations than as perfect models for educational renewal.

Defining what Black Power really means, actually and potentially, is an implicit aim of the book beginning with the Foreword, a speech presented by the author to an audience of more than 5,000 at the dedication of the new Malcolm X College.

The idea of the community college is discussed in some detail because it represents a major area of control over the education process by people of ethnic groups. More than 20 Black and Spanish-speaking presidents have been appointed in community colleges during the period 1968–71. At least three times as many more will be appointed before the end of 1975. Further, these colleges are becoming the real key to economic security.

Historically, the public community college movement in the United States, can be traced to Joliet, Illinois, where in 1901 the first two-year public college began operation. From 1902 through 1959, twenty additional two-year colleges were established in Illinois and were operated by local Boards of Education. Since 1960, thirty-six new two-year colleges have sprouted up around the state thus placing Illinois near the top of the national leadership in the community college movement but far behind California with its ninety or more.

Since the passage of the Illinois Public Junior College Act of 1965 which identified junior colleges with the system of higher education, only North Carolina has opened more public two-year colleges (24) than has Illinois (23). However, the twenty-three colleges in Illinois opened since 1966 enrolled 64,418 students for the Fall 1970 semester or four times the number of students enrolled in the North Carolina community colleges constructed after 1965. The total number of students enrolled in the fifty-seven private and public community colleges in Illinois as of October 1970 was 156,508 for an 8 percent increase over the 1969 enrollment.

Seven hundred and fifty two-year oriented programs are offered by the public community colleges in Illinois. The eight career divisions that encompass these seven hundred and fifty two-year programs are Agriculture, Business, Data Processing, Health-Medical, Public Social Service, Secretarial Technology, and Trades-Crafts. Of the 7,345 graduates of Illinois Public Junior Colleges in June, 1970, thirty-seven percent were trained in a career curriculum under the eight broad career divisions.

Instructional costs for students enrolled in a transfer oriented curriculum averaged between 1250–1350 dollars in Illinois in 1970. The average instructional costs per full-time-equivalent (FTE) student enrolled in occupational programs was in 1970 1600–1800 dollars.

In Illinois, by law, community college tuition cannot exceed one-third of instructional costs. Average tuition for community college students, by state, ranks Illinois among the sixteen states that charge the lowest tuition. Average tuition for Illinois Public community college is $195; however, for 1971–72, average tuition costs per FTE will increase to $225. The city of Chicago has continued to maintain a tuition-free status for local students although demands for tuition are becoming more vociferous at every session of the state's General Assembly.

The approximately 20,000 Black students attending community colleges in Chicago in the fall of 1971 represented an increase of more than 400 percent in attendance at all undergraduate institutions five years earlier. Malcolm X, with approximately 8,000 Black youth enrolled, has the largest undergraduate enrollment of black students in the country. When one considers that only in the last decade 90 percent of all Black undergraduates were enrolled in "predominately Negro" southern colleges, the picture becomes even more dramatic. It is easy to project at this time a nation-wide enrollment of Black students in community colleges by 1975 exceeding 500,000, more than the total of all Black students presently attending all colleges and universities. The impact on the nation's four-year colleges and graduate schools is incalculable. *The implications for the economy may represent the major crisis of the second half of the seventies.*

There can be little doubt that even most community colleges as they now exist are irrelevant and often destructive to the Black community, in part because Blacks are taught to synthesize the experience and accept the conclusions of other people on an exclusive basis. The result ·is usually an acceptance by the Black student of white people's analyses and conclusions. He is promoted into solutions for his people contrived and stamped acceptable by another people.

Education for Black students now and for the future must make them consistently conscious of struggle and commitment. In addition to building an identity, it must aid them to understand and interpret their historical and cultural experiences from their own perspective. Above all they must engage the kinds of educational experiences that lead to professional and technical competence at the highest possible level of excellence without permitting it to detract from the supreme importance of humanity and the struggle to make justice the chief characteristic of the world we must build together.

Aiding those who would seek peaceful resolution of today's conflicts is the overwhelming sense of Black nationalism that has already begun to transform young Black America.

The Afro-hair style is a pronounced vote of confidence in the natural beauty of one's own physical qualities.

The Black power handshake is a sign of determined togetherness and mutual respect.

The adoption of the tri-color "Black" flag (red, black and green) is a symbol of a new spirit of independence and pride.

The various forms of creative expression in art, music, poetry, and dance; the rejection of integration as an urgent priority; the wearing of dashikis, bubas, and other forms of African style clothing; the pilgrimage to the continent of Africa, the emphasizing and legitimizing by Blacks with bachelors, masters, and PH.Ds of the language style unique to the Black community; the rise of the Dick Gregorys, the Charles Koens, the Muhammad Alis, the Shirley Chisholms, and the Angela Davises as heroes and heroines; the prolonged rebellions such as Cairo, Illinois; the occupation by the Republic of New Africa (RNA) of land in Bolton, Mississippi; an explosion of talent in baseball, football, and basketball; an Arthur Ashe to blaze the way in tennis, a Charlie Sifford in golf; a rededicated Sammy Davis, Jr.; a humanitarian

Nancy Wilson; an evangelistic Aretha Franklin; a Julian Bond, a John Conyers, a John Cashin, and a Jessie Jackson; a Ralph Metcalfe, a George Collins, an Andrew Hatcher, a Carl Stokes, an Edward Brooke; and then the hundreds of thousands of heroes on every block of Black America's ghettoes quoting the poetry of Imamu Amir Baraka and Don Lee, buttressing new psychological strengths, validating the Black culture in their several ways, and inspiring in their presence countless others to feel that "we shall be free in this country one day . . . and we shall achieve our freedom by any means necessary."

*Those who make peaceful revolution impos-
sible make violent revolution inevitable.*
Ramsey Clark

1

THE EDUCATIONAL CRISIS

Black power, one of the healthiest and most legitimate developments in the history of America, has begun to force significant
changes on the American educational scene. None too soon,
most would now say, because the crisis in education has become
acute. If significant change does not occur, and soon, the institution of education may become one of the most repressive
forces in our society, instead of an instrument of liberation—as
we would have it.

To some extent education already is a contemporary mechanism for enslavement of seriously undereducated minority groups
in America.

The major aim of this book is to examine some chief reasons
for this repressive influence. Hopefully, we may forestall the
threatening collapse of this country's educational system by examining also some reasons for optimism emerging from the creative efforts of a relative few, and by proposing further some
steps that might brighten the future.

The idea that education is failing us is not new in itself. The
educational crisis in the United States as it affects all classes and

races has generated much negative opinion for some time, expressed during the '60s through a barrage of parental complaints and a variety of published studies, articles, and books.

The most dramatic statements concerning the problems contributing to education's current condition are coming from spokesmen for Black Americans, Chicanos, Puerto Ricans, Indians, and other neglected citizens.

Dan Aldridge, former head of the Detroit Chapter of SNCC (Student Non-Violent Coordinating Committee), describes schools in the Black communities, for example, as "red-light districts and . . . baby sitting compounds. . . . The critical condition," the angry Black community leader states, "involves not only corruption and deterioration . . . but the fact that Black youth are losing any desire to learn."

Lerone Bennett, the Black historian, makes the point that "In white-orientated schools, we are educated away from ourselves, away from our people, away from our rhythm, away from our soul. . . ."

Charles Silberman, author of *Crisis in the Classroom*, is typical, on the other hand, of the variety of white critics who also put their case dramatically. Silberman states unequivocally, for example, ". . . the schools are failing all of us. They are failing," he points out, "less because of maliciousness than because of *mindlessness*."

Some minority group spokesmen would not agree with that part of Silberman's premise concerning lack of maliciousness, but they would agree that failure or refusal to think seriously about educational purpose and reluctance to question and change established practice are prime factors in the failures that all are coming to recognize. They would contend also that a certain kind of "mindlessness" is diffused throughout the entire society, inclusive of education. Most importantly, they would argue that what tomorrow's world needs is not masses of intellectuals, as claimed by many with a classical view, but masses of people educated to feel and to act, as well as to think; people who are action-oriented humanists of the first order.

Our schools as now constituted are not prepared to meet this need.

A survey by Grace Boggs, an outstanding Black educator in Detroit, and the Silberman Report, referred to by some as a "scholastic horror story," are among the many publications of the '60s and the '70s making sweeping and thoroughly researched indictments of the public school system in the United States. Even these reports, however, shocking as they are, do not go far enough in documenting the particularly deplorable plight of education as it exists for the country's depressed minorities.

Rest rooms that are little more than state-financed narcotics distribution centers, former students who have been "pushed out" before graduation now "dropping-in" to engage in a plethora of illegal or disruptive activities—criminal assaults, vandalism, robberies, sales of "hot" merchandise,—all of these combine with nonresident teachers, who rush in and out of the community understanding little of its dynamics or its priority of concerns, to create an atmosphere of frustrated academic hopelessness.

The educational crisis has now become acute, threatening the very roots of the nation's ability to sustain itself. Preoccupation with other crises must not prevent action on the important and urgent defects of schools all over this nation.

Examining the crisis of education out of the context of existing social and political dilemmas that are a part of our time has already proved to be simply another exercise in futility. For this reason, this book will not only delve into the weaknesses of the educational system but also into the deteriorating social fabric which must be renewed if hope for improved educational processes is to exist.

It should not be surprising that little in all the available reports on the status of education, outside of the progressively deteriorating situation for Blacks, reds, and browns, was new. It is only surpising that so little has been done over the years as a result of the revelations. It has taken an educational revolution precipitated primarily by youthful Black dissidents to initiate some truly new beginnings, as discussed at a later point in this book.

Major findings that have been frustrating sensitive educators for years, but now being reported upon anew, are as follows:

1. The atmosphere in too many schools is intellectually sterile and aesthetically barren.

2. Large numbers of schools, most appreciably those in minority-group communities, are joyless places governed by oppressive and petty rules.

3. It is not possible to spend any prolonged period visiting public school classrooms without being appalled by the lack of such things as spontaneity, joy in learning, pleasure in creating, and any sense of self.

4. Students of all backgrounds and many educators are now rejecting the traditional myths about education that have encouraged a paranoiac resistance to change.

5. Most teachers have no understanding of education's historical role in America's past and do not have much, if any, insight into the role education should play in the future.

6. Teachers too often assume that pupils cannot be trusted to act in their own best interests and principals make similar assumptions about teachers.

7. Teachers and administrators, by practicing systematic repression, create many of their own discipline problems, while promoting docility, passivity, and conformity in the students.

8. Schools tend to discourage students from developing the capacity to learn by and for themselves because they are structured in such a way as to make students totally dependent upon teachers.

9. Most classes are taught in a uniform manner, without regard to the individual student's understanding of, or interest in, subjects that are often characterized by irrelevance, banality, and triviality.

10. The formal classroom produces its own discipline problems and promotes restlessness and various forms of misbehavior.

11.   Teacher gains through unionizing have stifled rather than encouraged willingness to expose the hypocrisies and inadequacies of the educational system.

12.   Too many teaching and administrative staff personnel come from outside the community, bringing with them the "missionary attitude" that they are "helping the backward natives," when in fact they are living off the natives.

In minority communities far too many students respond to these conditions by permitting themselves to be pushed out of school or by dropping out.

They flee the system and reject all it represents.

The suprise is, of course, that even more students do not rebel rather than accept the stultifying rules, the authoritarianism, the boring lack of inspiration, the generally depressing conditions, and the abuse of power one sees throughout education.

Perhaps most threatening of all to our future as a nation are the limitations of existing schools that deny students a needed ability to understand complex modern phenomena and to translate that understanding into action. In order to acquire those abilities needed by citizens of the future, students must learn far more than the basic skills of scholarship taught in a repressive classroom atmosphere. Education must prepare people not just to earn a living, but to live as creative, dignified, and sensitive human beings.

For the adults of tomorrow nothing is more impractical than an education designed only to prepare them for specific vocations or professions, or to facilitate their adjustment to the world only as it is today.

Black students in particular are expressing the belief that their education must prepare them for survival as Black people with a strong sense of humanity, and for work that does not yet exist and whose nature cannot even be imagined. The required preparation, they feel, can be achieved only by teaching them how to learn on their own, and by giving them the kind of intellectual stimulation that will develop their ability to apply man's accumulated wisdom to new problems as they arise.

Essentially, all of this may be interpreted to mean that to meet the challenges now emerging the schools must become instruments for humanizing people as well as teaching them to be technically or professionally competent.

Under existing conditions it seems almost absurd to hope that schools can become a humane instrument for humanizing people and educate well at the same time. Even the task of becoming student-centered and subject- or knowledge-centered at the same time may be expecting too much.

Yet, there *is* ample reason to hope that the schools can place more emphasis on aesthetic and moral factors and create greater intellectual excellence as a result.

The kind of education being sought by protesting students is, however, in no way synonymous with schooling as we know it today. To provide the humanizing experiences being demanded, as well as the means to technical competence, the very face of education must change.

Students in the future must be encouraged to learn as much if not more outside than inside the formal classrooms. To create the environment being sought, education must recruit available help from outside itself but within its community. Proper weight must be given, in other words, to *all* the other educating sources in American society: work, television, films, the mass media, churches and synagogues, the law, medicine and health care, museums and libraries, the armed forces, corporate training programs, and various informal youth activities.

The educational system must at the same time take steps to revolutionize teacher attitudes and upgrade their preparation.

Most teachers are victimized almost as much as the students by the current state of education. Lacking any considered philosophy of education, teachers of today tend to do primarily what teachers before them have done. They seldom question established practice. In the rare instances when they do, it seldom progresses beyond the stage of lip service.

Twelve years of dull, repressive formal public schooling, four years of uninspired formal college, and one year at the master's level do little to prepare a creative teacher who can innovate with authority. This is another important fact we must face.

Complicating life for minority students all over the country is the presence of too many middle-class oriented teachers who have not been educated to think seriously about the purposes and consequences of what they are trying to do, especially in terms of the relationship of educational means to ends.

While the inadequacies of existing teacher education programs are more serious for teachers of minorities and the poor of all descriptions, the preparation of few if any teachers in middle-class, suburban schools may be considered even remotely adequate.

Encouragingly in all of this the massive criticism heaped upon education, educators, and teacher-preparation institutions during the past several decades has begun to sensitize various publics concerning the issues to the extent that an unprecedented effort to support massive changes is becoming evident.

Angry parents are becoming more determined. Irritated employees are becoming more critical. Harassed taxpayers are demanding more accountability. The future, therefore, may not be as gloomy as present circumstances tend to predict.

In fact, hope for relief from the gloomy portraits of education provided by such observers as Lewis Mayhew, Grace Boggs, James Coleman, Preston Wilcox, Bobbie Wright, Charles Silberman, Barbara Sizemore, Clark Kerr, and hundreds of thousands of disappointed parents is already being provided to some degree by a relatively few promising models of reform scattered across the country. Some of these models are even encouraging freedom, informality, and individuality, taking great care to avoid the lack of concern with subject matter and intellectual discipline that many believe drove the progressive movement of the '20s and '30s into disrepute.

Many more educators than at present would probably be receptive to new approaches and reform if they were given the necessary encouragement and support by parents, other taxpayers, and business leaders. Their reluctance to innovate reflects the reasons why substantial attitudinal changes must be effected within the structure of education and throughout the society. Such a condition may now be on the threshold of reality.

A slowly emerging national mood supporting change is becoming apparent. And, despite well-known criticisms, the technological revolution that brought us cybernetics, automation, and the ability to conquer space is now being viewed by some as being among the strongest nonideological underpinnings of new hopes for the future. Our ability to humanize technology as well as ourselves may become the supreme test.

In any event, new hope for the future certainly cannot be based on illusions built around ill-conceived plans of "compensatory" or "remedial" education which encourage notions of racial inferiority. Such programs are psychologically, intellectually, and morally destructive. They promote conflict, without speaking to main issues contributing to the country's failure to develop the majority of its human potential.

Neither will constructive change result from naive belief in the possibility of "miracle" programs. Miracles just don't happen in education. Premature elation over initial results from Head Start, Job Corps, and other less glamorous efforts created new problems, while only obscuring the real issues surrounding old ones.

The programs did, however, teach us a great deal about what not to do or expect, as well as a great deal more about pathways of fruitful potential for educating people. They provided foundations on which truly effective programs of education can be built.

On the practical level, many educators are now becoming aware that need for more individual attention to students and more concentration on human factors may be possible only through learning more about how to relegate routine detail and information processing to technological innovations. Even as it too has retreated from "miracle" status, educational technology stands revealed now as a highly promising source of assistance for creative educators given the chance to create.

Most importantly, some sensitive Black educators are spearheading efforts toward a revolution in education that has direction and substance. Focusing attention on the specific faults of education as they now exist, these educational leaders are calling for increased community control, a redefinition of educational purpose, more accountability and responsiveness, and the elimination of obsolescence, insensitivity, and racist practices.

The existence of a new mood for change in education is being accelerated in the United States by what is going on in the rest of the world. Creative experiments with innovations have already begun to abound in countries from Asia to Africa, to the future good of us all. The fact that the United States is not leading most of the trends toward change is encouraging rather than otherwise.

While participating in a world conference on education sponsored by the World Council of Churches at Bergen Au Zee, the Netherlands, this writer was surprised at the world-wide progress (by the African countries, in particular) in educational innovation and relevance. Although the idea of national assessment of the schools as a corollary to national reforms in other areas is only now gaining momentum in the United States, it has become a well-established practice in many other countries from whom we could learn much.

Governments in Albania, Brazil, Ghana, Iceland, Romania, Spain, Yugoslavia, France, Panama, and Trinidad have already developed educational policy plans intimately related to a national program for their own unique, overall social and economical development. Similarly in Japan, Thailand, Turkey, and the United Arab Republic, "high councils" or "central committees" oversee school needs and maintain their relevance to national needs and goals while encouraging maximum autonomy at the "local" levels.

Sweden, the Ivory Coast, and Spain have created new central educational research institutions for essentially the same reasons as we need one in the U.S.

A majority of African nations, most impressively Tanzania, are aiming new school programs toward the improvement of agriculture and rural trades as a national economic as well as a social necessity. In Guiana, Thailand, and Turkey, the major goal is production of middle-level manpower for the same reasons. In Algeria, the Sudan, Tanzania, Malaysia, and Singapore, the strengthening of the language base in education is being given primacy as a national priority.

Many countries are also experimenting with changes in the structure and organization of schools. Their reasons are pragmatic:

    1.   Growing populations and a shortage of money

    2.   Teachers and school facilities that thwart efforts to improve or expand educational opportunity

    3.   Educational systems that cannot achieve the goals set by the nation

    4.   Excessive school dropouts

    5.   Lack of balance among the several sectors of education

    6.   An important gap between what these societies expect of their schools and what the schools are in fact delivering.

The Netherlands Conference also revealed an emerging tendency to regard curriculum development as a continuous process: a world-wide emphasis on new approaches to teaching mathematics, science, and languages; liberalized views concerning the nature of human potential and capability; and a corresponding tendency to increase the learning load of students, while making the entire educational scene more flexible.

Many foreign educators spoke also of making far more extensive use of educational television and computers as valid aids for teaching. Much of this work is still at a research and development stage.

Interestingly, innovation and experimentation are not restricted to any particular grade level in most countries.

Pre-primary schooling, similar in concept to the U.S. "Head Start" program, is receiving determined interest on an experimental basis throughout the world, especially in Germany, Italy, Israel, the Soviet Union, England, and Korea, as well as in the developing nations of Mali and Lebanon.

At the secondary level, experimentation is underway in the

area of reconciling more efficiently the function of the school at this level with the occupational needs of the society, while at the same time meeting the demands of preparation for the collegiate level.

Educators at the Bergen conference were unanimous in agreeing that secondary schools must continue striving for a more modern content related to life and to work at the same time.

Some nations are already spurring a better coordination of learning between secondary schools and the job market. Others are successfully blurring the line between high school and college. Improved student guidance and experiments with new school forms such as a preuniversity "Kolleg" in Austria and the international movement towards community colleges are related to these efforts.

Some of the nations mentioned, like certain areas in the United States, are experimenting with school calendar changes to intensify class work and make fuller use of school facilities. These include Hungary, Yugoslavia, Argentina, and Ecuador.

Canada, Spain, and the Soviet Union are trying to provide more efficient educational services by deliberately increasing the size of schools, creating regional schools, and closing small local schools.

England has taken the leadership in expanding the "college without walls" concept in a most exciting way by creating the "Open College" or "Free University." This latest version of a college without a campus deserves careful study.

Another striking international "reform" is the growth of student participation in government, with functions ranging from advisory to deliberative. Decentralization of educational policymaking to include students raises hopes for more flexibility in every aspect of school operation.

Throughout the world it appears, student unrest as a characteristic of the '60s set the stage for sweeping reforms in the '70s. In Sweden, student councils are now obligatory in all upper secondary schools. In France and Italy they are provided for in official school regulations.

It becomes obvious when examining the world situation that

America can no longer afford to be victimized by immobility in
its educational system. And the evidence slowly but irrepressibly
coming to view is that the country is becoming aware and doing
something about it.

One sign of progress in education was provided through an
announcement by the Department of Health, Education, and
Welfare that the Federal government would begin helping set
up a "college without walls" arrangement under which one student can attend several colleges during his four undergraduate
years without penalty. The idea is to free students from traditional university residence requirements and give them greater
latitude to follow their interests. In addition to giving students
more freedom to transfer, the plan is designed to let them do
more work for course credit outside formal institutional settings.

At the opposite end of the educational spectrum activity is
also generating.

More than 6,000 school children in grades K-8 of Valley View
School District 96, Romeoville, Illinois, now attend classes
throughout the calendar year, including the months of July and
August. This revolutionary school calendar has increased the utilization of school buildings by one-third, and has already saved
the school district more than $5 million in new construction
costs.

Another educational innovation, the Voucher Plan, discussed
theoretically for some time, began receiving its test by fire in
1970 in the United States. The plan made it possible for parents,
regardless of income, to select what they considered the best
school for their children. Parents received education vouchers
amounting to the sum the community spends on each public
school pupil; they took the vouchers to any participating school
—public, parochial, or private—and enrolled their children.

The plan ran into opposition on various grounds:

1. It might encourage the creation of all-Black or all-
white schools.

2. It might lead to direct public support of church-
related schools.

3. Public schools might become dumping grounds for children not wanted by other schools.

4. It might bring about the establishment of fly-by-night schools.

All of these are silly bugaboos which say a great deal about the mentality of those controlling or affecting decisions about the education of children and youth in America.

Advocates of the Plan have injected specific requirements designed to prevent materialization of these problems. It is still too early to evaluate the success of the program. The possibility that it may not achieve its objectives resides more in a lack of determination to make it work rather than in the weaknesses set forth by critics.

Even more controversial is the idea of performance contracting on a guaranteed basis by private companies. One firm has contracted with the Federal government to provide tutoring in both reading and math in a nationwide network of 77 centers that offer tutoring at five dollars an hour. The subdued surroundings of these private centers—carpeting, drapes, fresh paint, and air conditioning—also include a so-called space-age approach to learning. The student's developmental needs are determined exclusively by an NCR Mark IV computer, which interprets the results of each student's comprehensive entrance test and then spins out "individually prescribed programmed instruction." The student then takes a lesson on an audiovisual reader (a Language Master, or some other kind of autotutor). He is presented in this way with a relatively new learning environment, subject to his immediate control. The atmosphere contains little to remind him of the traditional classroom where failure was the order of the day.

Also under a Federal grant, Massachusetts brought in Educational Solutions, Inc., of New York in an experimental attempt to upgrade the reading skills of some 400 pupils at Boston's predominantly Black Dearborn Elementary School. Less involved with hardware than Learning Foundations, this company offered a special, copyrighted words-in-color reading program and provided the teachers with training, instructional material, and counseling throughout the school year.

Despite the controversy and the many apparent hazards, performance contracting is in for an extended trial.

In Gary, Indiana, the entire operation of one of Gary's elementary schools was turned over in September 1970 to Behavioral Research Laboratories for a fee of $800 per pupil, equal to what Gary spends annually on each inner-city child. BRL concentrates on the fundamentals of reading and math before going on to other subjects. In its contract with the Gary school board, BRL agreed to refund its $2,400 fee for each student who, after three years, is not learning at accepted national norms, as reflected by independent tests.

As a result of this contract, the school temporarily lost its accreditation by the Indiana State Board of Education. Why this happened even temporarily is very hard to understand in the light of the facts of life as they exist today in education for most Americans. "Problems" disconcerting to the State were: The use of nonstate-certified teachers and use of a curriculum emphasizing math and reading instead of a "balanced curriculum" which also incorporated science, social studies, and health. Use of nonstate-approved textbooks, violation of state-set teacher-pupil ratios, and delegation of authority for running the Banneker Elementary School to BRL's administrator instead of the school's principal were also cited as significant factors in the disaccreditation.

All of the objections by the state are irrelevant. Their citation simply documents the narrow perspective within which most of education operates. The Gary program's early success tends to prove this.

The first really large performance contracting program in a single school system was started in Philadelphia, where a private firm was given the task of improving the reading ability of 15,000 children. This district also contracted with Behavioral Research Laboratories to raise the reading level of 14,500 elementary children and 500 junior high students by at least one year. The contract provided for $600,000 (or $40 per student) if the firm succeeded. Their responsibility included providing instructional materials, training teachers and paraprofessionals, and interpreting the program to the community. Here again it is too early for a valid evaluation, but the outlook is good if the usual forms of resistance to change can be overcome.

Still another promising approach to revitalizing the educational process as it affects the poor and the minorities is the community school (not to be confused with the community college, although some aspects of philosophy are similar.) Marked by maximum local control and decentralization, nongraded divisions, heavy emphasis on developing individual potential, individualized learning formats, classrooms without walls, and full integration of all community resources in a concentrated effort to meet educational needs, the community school can be the instrument of responsiveness needed in contemporary urban settings.

The term "community school" is disturbing to some, confusing to others. These attitudes result because of a tendency to force the community school concept into institutional patterns as they currently exist in education.

Schools operated through an absentee administration, only remotely familiar with the specific characteristics of a particular neighborhood, can never be absorbed into the conceptual frame of reference constituting the idea of a community school. Neither is a situation tolerable where teachers "rush in" from the outlands (the suburbs) to occupy the school building for a specified number of hours. The pattern of alien "rush ins" who "rush out" with frantic haste at the closing bell is one of the major reasons for the general hostility existing now between the school and the Black community.

The true community school provides built-in safety features to handle its own failures; staffing patterns that blur the lines demarcating professional and nonprofessional staff and formal and informal staff; procedures to permit community participation in the accrediting process, as well as in all others; indigenous counseling and instructional personnel; meaningful curricula that can respond swiftly to new events and ideas; up to 24 hours a

day and seven days a week participation in community development.

The question of whether the community school begins at the
kindergarten or some earlier or later grade is irrelevant. In its to-
tality it may begin as early as age two and encompass the educational needs of the community at the post-baccalaureate level.
In essence, as we could conceive it now, the community school
(including college) would begin as an alternative system com-
peting with the present one to fill its voids and compensate for
its weaknesses. It would become, in a sense, the communiversity
of the people, an educational ideal to meet the diverse needs of
a contemporary society where education is a right for every individual.

Again, however, the road to any educational ideal will not be
an easy one, for the barriers are many. The last decade has wit-
nessed some increased willingness to redistribute the power of
central school boards, but not enough. Paradoxically, while rural
areas still struggle with issues of consolidation, some cities are
seeking viable ways to decentralize. So far, most efforts have
proved a decisive political failure, as in New York, and it may be
some time before the idea of community control can gain momentum. The Chicago plan for redistribution of power over education is a dubious one, already under attack and designed to
fail.

In some large cities, including Chicago, where Malcolm X
College is experimenting on a massive basis, another dynamic
effort is underway to decentralize the school system from below
in the form of the storefront school, or "street academy."

The concept of the street academy derived partially from economic and physical necessity, but more significantly, from a belief that schools should be only a step from the street. When the
distance between the community and the school is a chasm, all
intimacy is lost. This is why ghetto schools have only a fragile
hold on their students. If the realities of his life are ignored, even
the possibility of tenuous communication with the student is ultimately lost.

Storefront schools have so far been primarily but not exclusively for high school dropouts. So that he can achieve his education goals, whatever they are, the academies are shaped by needs of the youth and are responsive to his aspirations.

Thirteen such academies were initiated in New York under the direction of Livingston Wingate, the astute director of the New York Urban League. Other cities have their own versions, with styles differing substantially. The major objective is the same— namely, helping students attain a meaningful education as defined by the student and local citizens.

One of the anticipated and hoped-for success signals of these academies has been a growing cooperation between them and boards of education. This is encouraging because it may be unreasonable to expect business and individuals to give financial support to such schools as street academies indefinitely or on a large scale. The street academy is an educational model. For its methods to be considered successful the academy must eventually be incorporated into the established public school system without being corrupted.

St. Louis has developed a plan now being emulated by a number of large school systems. Through grants from the Rockefeller Foundation and the Danforth Foundation, as well as by expenditures of local tax funds, the St. Louis Board of Education has launched a major program of community schools for youth and adults. The Model Cities Program has entered into an extensive agreement with the Board of Education for shared responsibilities in expanding community schools in which local citizens hold decision-making powers. Each year, an advisory parent-teacher congress in every district assumes increased responsibility and authority.

The St. Louis Board of Education, a neighborhood group, and the Danforth Foundation in the summer of 1969 shared in financing a neighborhood summer school directed and staffed by the Association of Black Collegians, Sophia Study Center. Initially, a tutorial center in the inner city, it has received two grants from the Danforth Foundation in the amount of $37,500 to extend its operations to include activities typical of the "street academy." The Center has been named by the Board as a branch

of one of the local high schools and assumes the formal responsibility of teaching certain skills and disciplines to youth who
spend one-half day in a public high school and one-half day at
the Study Center.

The Olatunji Center, a street academy in East St. Louis,
funded by the Lutheran Inner-City Ministry and the Danforth
Foundation, includes students and parents on its board and is attempting to devise a curricular program unique for its own student body. Through the route of tests of General Education
Development, the Center seeks to prepare individuals for admission to college.

None of the programs described negates the proposition by
Aldridge: "It is already much too late for such band-aids as more
money, or more police, or more schools, or more parent involve-
ments, or more teachers, or more time in school." The Black and
other minority communities cannot afford the luxury of further
indulgence in myths and promises that have no meaning.

Realization of what must be done is slowly becoming evident
even at the level of the President of the United States. Possibly
the most important of the new messages on education in America is contained in the 1970 report of the President's Task Force
on Higher Education, entitled, *Priorities in Higher Education*,
which reads as follows:

> While recognizing that the diversity of American higher edu-
> cation is a central part of its strength and that no single report
> can speak for all American colleges and universities, we are in
> unanimous agreement in emphasizing the importance of increas-
> ing support for higher education as a fundamental national re-
> source if we are to realize more fully the promise of American
> life. To lessen the capacity or equality of higher education would
> be to lessen America's ability to respond to the whole range of
> problems at home and abroad for which skilled manpower,
> trained intellect, and creative imagination are critical.
>
> For both the near-term, and especially the long-term needs of
> this nation, we urge that no immediate pressure be allowed to
> erode the quality or potentials of colleges and universities as
> strong, independent centers of learning and of free and objective
> inquiry.

We wish to emphasize, however, that not all individuals should be encouraged to seek the same post-high school educational goals. From vocational training to advanced graduate and professional programs, many individual capabilities and needs must be recognized and served realistically.

If we fail to observe these differences among people and do not provide a variety of optimum opportunities to match them, and if we do not oppose pressures that encourage the pursuit of status rather than substance, we will only erode the quality of post-high school educational institutions of all types.

All but one of our members are unanimous in urging that federal financial support for specific purpose in higher education, public and private, be substantially increased . . . all believe that the Federal government must undertake specific expansions if the needs of Americans are to be met.

We are unanimous in recognizing that our colleges and universities have major internal responsibilities to clarify their individual purposes and functions and to increase the effectiveness of their operations and governance. In addition to recommending federal priorities, we have defined critical institutional priorities.

The following are, in our opinion, the most immediate Federal priorities:

Financial aid for disadvantaged students
Support for health care professional education
Increased tax incentives for support to higher education.

We believe the following are Continuing Federal Priorities:

The expansion of opportunities for post-high school education
The support of high quality graduates and professionals.

We believe four areas constitute the higher Institutional Priorities for our colleges and universities:

Clarification of institutional purposes
Improvement in the quality of the curriculum and methods of
    teaching and learning
More efficient use of resources
Clarification of institutional governance.

While such questions as these must be answered by each institution for itself, we believe it would be highly useful for the nation that there be established a *National Academy of Higher Education*, independent of Government but federally chartered, on the model of the National Academy of Science, which the Congress and President Lincoln inaugurated a century ago. The Academy should serve as a national center to which questions of this kind can be referred for thoughtful and continuing study.

There is now no single nongovernmental agency devoted specifically to the analysis of the problem of higher education as a national resource, and we strongly believe that there should be such an Academy.

In summary, we believe the primary federal objectives in higher education should be:

(1) To make appropriate educational opportunities available to all those who are qualified

(2) To sustain high-quality centers of academic excellence throughout America.

The overwhelming majority of the members of our Task Force are convinced that the present level of educational opportunities for economically disadvantaged students and the present financial condition of our institutions of higher education, both public and private, require a major increase in federal support designed to serve these specific purposes.

In summary, six highly encouraging factors, in addition to the report by the President's Task Force, document the validity for hope here in the United States.

First is the evolution of the community school or college as a legitimate institution for ministering to the educational ills of a community.

Second is the highly substantive report on "Priorities" issued by the Carnegie Commission, and the possibility of a new kind of moral leadership for all of education.

Third is the breakthrough of such new curriculum areas as Black Studies, Chicano Studies, Ethnic Studies, Urban Studies, Latin-American Studies, and Non-Western Studies.

Fourth are new views in the areas of governance, human potential, variation in learning styles, structural relationships within educational institutions, and a new capacity for self-criticism by the schools, themselves.

Fifth is the urban unrest which must be viewed as a positive force.

Sixth is the wide-spread attention being called to the incidence and impact of racism on this country's institutions and its people.

The major aim of this book is to explore the dimensions of each of these critical factors in the educational revolution many hope will explode education out of its atavistic tendency to resist creative change.

Despite the expressed high hopes for progress in the near future, it is still necessary to examine in sufficient depth socioeconomic and sociopolitical factors contributing to the present state of affairs in education as a basis for change.

Realizing that all is not sweetness and light is a necessary first step in forming new determinations. Only through examination of the environmental context can we understand existing urgencies. Moreover, the logical reordering of priorities is a natural outgrowth of these same understandings.

Socrates once observed, "Our conversation is not about something casual, but about the proper way of life." What we do in education as teachers and students must be judged by society in the light of our quest for a proper and appropriate way of life.

It is society's responsibility to postulate man, not as he has been, or even as he is, but as he can be. The task of a nation is to educate men and women to be understanding human beings who respect the sanctity of life and the dignity of all other human beings. That's what an education for humanism is all about. The problems are many, and they are complexly diverse. Yet, in the words of Martin Luther King, "We shall overcome," and, in the words of Malcolm X, "By any means necessary . . . as long as [the means] are intelligently directed and designed to get results."

*Morality is the basis of things and truth is
the substance of all morality. . . . As soon as we
lose the moral basis, we cease to be religious.
. . . Man cannot be untruthful, cruel, or inconti-
nent and claim to have God on his side.*
Mohandas Karamchand (Mahatma) Gandhi

2

THE MORAL CHALLENGE

The United States is experiencing unprecedented moral confusion and demoralizing conflict among its people. This is a
prime factor in the dilemma of education.

Perhaps the most important single explanation of *why* the
country has been in this kind of trouble for a decade or more
lies in one of the major reasons for turbulence on the educational scene: the absence, in a contemporary sense, of a clearly
defined and accepted social and humanistic mission for American education. A direct outgrowth is a corresponding inability on
the part of the educational enterprise to implant an appropriate
sense of ethics in its products, the students.

Lewis Mayhew, in his book *Colleges Today and Tomorrow,*
takes this position: "A weakening or a failure of Judeo–Christian
theology must be assigned some force for . . . conflicts [and]
other paradoxes in American life. . . . [Educational] institutions
have been unable to take and maintain a strong moral stand . . .
partly because their own moral position was assailable. . . ."

It can be no wonder that the country, as well as its schools,
has been beset by innumerable conflicts. The important objec-

tives of human existence and a universally acceptable system of human values remain ill defined and confused in the minds of most citizens.

The schools may be held largely responsible also for our pres- ent debilitating moral crises as they extend even into interna- tional affairs.

One has to realize that it is the educated man who has put us where we are today. The rape of Vietnam was begun by so-called liberally educated men, not by school dropouts. Pollution of the environment is carried out by men educated at the best scientific and technical centers, not by fools and idiots.

It seems fair to contend on the basis of available evidence that the failure to develop a contemporary ethic upon which an honest morality structure can be built has left this country in a state where racism, paternalism, materialism, and repression su- persede all else. At the same time concern is almost nonexistent for such values as human life, human dignity, the unimpeded opportunity to pursue happiness, and preservation of the natural environment.

Chief among the critical moral issues ripping apart the na- tion's fabric, as the Rev. Jesse Jackson has emphasized repeat- edly, are the continuing conflicts between Black and white Amer- icans and the inequalities of existence prevalent for millions who are poor and underprivileged.

The racial crisis, above all others, has become an integral part of the basic crises of values gathering momentum in American society and has contributed greatly to the turbulence in the schools and in the streets.

There can be no doubt that our failure to cope with the pres- ent panorama of problems, frightening in their potential, is rap- idly leading us to the ultimate moment of truth about our future existence.

The major question has now become whether the country shall or shall not survive.

Certainly, if we are unable to do something impressive about the increasing human conflicts and the overwhelming waste of our human potential, we face the danger of ultimate destruction from the sheer weight of accumulated frustrations.

The problems are three-fold: (1) A kind of spoliation of the humanity-potential in our society through disordered priorities, excessive stress on material things, and a faulty system of values; (2) Failure to provide adequate developmental opportunities for too many millions of our people, particularly Black and other minority group persons; (3) An unwillingness by the managers of our society to exercise social responsibility in matters that promote racism and pollute the natural and human environments.

There is a need now for our national leaders to begin realizing that human potential and what we do with it is intimately involved with the total environment in which humanity is attempting to survive and with our ability to do so. In consequence, a new sense of moral responsibility must redirect a significant share of our intellectual genius toward developing new theories of human reconciliation.

We must also begin to understand that schools and other formal institutions which cannot constantly reshape themselves to become harmonious with an ever-changing life environment will become obsolete and eventually serve destructive rather than constructive ends.

And finally, it must become apparent to the leaders of America that education, higher education in particular, is the most powerful instrument our society possesses for effecting positive social change. It must be used for this purpose.

Certainly the legitimacy of the position stated here is well established. The basic function of education has always been to liberate men. Education has performed this function in the past by adapting itself to the problems men have faced. The current challenge, more monumental than ever in the past, is a burden that threatens education's ability to deliver, and yet deliver it must.

The whole mentality of our society must undergo constant restructuring stimulated by education, and if the effort does not succeed, there is little hope we can confront the current crises with optimism for the future. And above all there must be a recognition that racism in the American economy remains as the most persistent and dangerous enemy of any hopes for domestic tranquility.

The United States, in principle, professes to be a country where there is liberty, freedom, and justice for all. In statements of public policy, it constantly reaffirms its stand against discrimination with regard to race, creed, color, and national origin. It reiterates time after time that all men are created equal, and that in this country advancement is based on personal merit rather than the color of one's skin. All of this sounds good but it is far from fact.

The challenge for America continues to be giving 23 million Black people—children, youth and adults—the same chance as white Americans to learn and grow, to work and share in society's benefits, to develop their abilities—physical, mental, and spiritual—and to engage in the pursuit of individual happiness, unimpeded by unfair practices of discrimination.

Despite peaceful protests and repeated marches, the Black American continued, in the 1960s, to find his pursuit of justice totally thwarted. The reaction should have been predictable. Black Americans became filled, understandably, with angry indignation and impatience. In cities all over the country they began in the latter half of the 60s to add new dimensions to the Nation's crises by shedding the old vestiges of submission, unending patience, and compromise. They are becoming imbued now in the 1970s with the cynical belief that full citizenship, demanded though it may be, is not marked for delivery tomorrow.

Young Americans of African descent are bitter. Many are refusing to salute the flag. They refuse also to show any sign of respect for the National Anthem and look upon loyalty to traditional American ideals as a form of betrayal of the Black community. This dangerous state of affairs represents "tinderbox potential" in the atmosphere of "superpatriotism" inspired by some white Americans, victimized themselves by a system which molded them into bigots, racists, or worse.

A study by Pierre deVise, a sociologist at De Paul University, presented some startling facts which make the City of Chicago an example of what is going wrong all over this land. In Chicago, one of the most, if not the most, segregated large cities in the United States, about 70 percent of the city's Blacks live in contiguous neighborhoods that are 90 percent or more Black. Another 28 percent live in neighborhoods that are on their way to becoming all Black. Only 2 percent live in stable, predominately white neighborhoods, a concentration "unprecedented in the history of American society."

In neighborhoods in transition from white to Black, rents become depressed as whites begin to leave. But later, as Blacks take over completely, rents for the now dilapidated housing not only recover but usually surpass the earlier ones. The incoming Blacks earn less than the whites they displace; thus the socioeconomic rank of the area goes down and the services provided by the City deteriorate correspondingly.

Compared to white housing, the average Black-occupied housing unit in Chicago during 1970 was:

     half as likely to be owner occupied

     five times more dilapidated

     three times more substandard

     four times more overcrowded.

Despite huge differences in income, Blacks pay as much as whites for unequal packages of housing.

About 87 percent of Black families spend one-fourth or more of their budget on rent; 36 percent of Black families spend over 35 percent. It is hardly likely that Blacks would voluntarily pay a housing premium of 15 percent, on the average, to live in a slum, not to speak of the other penalties of Black ghetto living, such as second-rate health services and almost nonexistent recreational facilities.

The findings of the deVise study show also that the socioeconomic and geographic gaps between whites and Blacks, and between rich and poor, already wide, are increasing in alarming proportions, despite various claims of agencies to the contrary in and out of the Federal government. Average Black family income has managed to remain at about two-thirds of white income only because the number of workers per Black family has been increasing faster than for whites. The ten poorest communities in metropolitan Chicago have one-fifth the average family income of the ten richest communities, compared to one-third back in 1950. All ten poor communities are in the west and southside Black ghettos of Chicago, while the ten richest communities are all in white suburbs in the north.

Chicago is not alone. Examination of the records of any major city show that the ignoble record of white America in her treatment of Black America is actually getting worse with each passing day, rather than better as some would have us believe.

According to the U. S. Department of Labor, unemployment in the poorest neighborhoods of the nation's 100 largest cities climbed by more than one-third during 1970. The number of unemployed persons in poverty neighborhoods averaged 510,000 in the third quarter of 1971, up by about 150,000 from the third quarter of 1969. The situation was worse among Black teenagers, whose jobless rate rose to more than 35 percent.

Jobless rates for Blacks in poverty neighborhoods were up sharply in 1971 over 1969. In some Black neighborhoods upwards of 85 percent of all employable youth were idle, festering in the futility of their aimless existence.

Although the present discussion concentrates on the plight of people of African origin in America, the situation for other minorities cannot add to the national pride.

The tragedy for the American Indian, for example, has been brutally shocking. The Northwest Territory Ordinance of 1787 states:

"The utmost good faith shall always be observed toward the Indians; their land and property shall never be taken from them without their consent; . . . laws founded in justice and humanity shall from time to time be made for preventing wrongs being done to them. . . ." This was the first full statement of U. S. Indian policy. But few, if any, national pledges have been so poorly honored.

Instead, the American Indians have been oppressed and brutalized, deprived of their ancestral lands and denied the opportunity to control their own destiny. The less than a million Indians now living on reservations or in urban slums are indeed among the country's most deprived and isolated minority groups.

Indians as tribes and individuals are living under a suffocating pattern of paternalism. Unemployment among Indians is ten times the national average; 80 percent of reservation Indians have incomes that fall below the poverty line. Average schooling for all Indians totals only six years. Their infant death rate is 70 percent higher than that of the general population, and the first Americans rank last by almost every other health standard.

Can it still be a surprise to anyone in the light of these facts that the Indian reservations and the urban reservations where the vast majority of Black and brown people are confined are hotbeds of social pathology—marked by high crime rates, serious problems of mental health, excessive numbers of school dropouts, and a myriad of other related social problems.

The seething hostility which has generated among all racial minorities grows out of the conviction that existing conditions for Black, red, and brown America prevail only because white America does not care.

Reasons for this belief stem from the peculiar willingness of the American public to give support most readily to proposals for increased numbers of police, rather than for better recreation centers, schools and housing.

There is, then, basis for the indignation expressed by the Black community. Even the most casual observation reveals that most middle-class white Americans—victims of their own thoughtlessness, and horribly deluded by a press that in many cases fails to meet its social responsibility—exhibits a dangerous naivete about racism and a distasteful lip service to a philosophy of human rights in which their actions demonstrate no sincere belief.

Surely Black Americans have a right to believe that the lady of justice permits the blindfold to slip over both eyes when her face is turned toward them, an action taken with the implied consent of a white-dominated power structure.

It is hard for Black Americans to understand *why* so many

white Americans have not taken the trouble to seek out the truth. The most frequent reason expressed is that white people really don't want to know and, as a result, are not forced to acknowledge the facts of life in the United States as they exist for millions of neglected fellow Americans.

Not knowing and not caring, Blacks believe, has become a habit of convenience for white Americans; it is an ostrich stance that must be uprooted if the nation is to survive.

Earl Warren, former U. S. Chief Justice, in October 1970, reminding the nation that 23 million Black people are still struggling for full educational, voting and human rights, said, "The violence (by whites) implicit in these denials . . . has provoked counterviolence (by Blacks) in many quarters, and the time has come when the nation must restore good will and cooperation regardless of race or color if we are to be a healthy nation."

Warren asserted that the basis of the problem has now become "bitterness" on both sides, and no solution is possible until this bitterness is removed. "It, therefore, seems clear to me," he said, "that if we are ever to have a placid nation again, at least during the lifetimes of our children and their children, it will be necessary for us to set aside our prejudices on account of race or color, and be willing to live in a plural society where American citizenship means, in fact as well as in precept, that all men are created equal and as such are entitled to life, liberty, and the pursuit of happiness."

He commented also about the 400,000 American Indians who are chafing openly about their ill treatment over past decades, along with 1,500,000 Asiatics and several millions of Latin–American ancestry who have felt many of the indignities that are prevalent against the Black people.

The heavy influx of Black people, as well as Puerto Ricans, Chicanos, and other minorities into the cities, may not be considered in itself, however, responsible for today's urban woes. Although most of the human casualties of today are found in largest numbers among the latecomers who experience rejection and hostility, the basic cause of the urban dilemma lies in the fact that officials and more affluent citizens alike did not plan for the future with determination and vigor.

Efforts to overcome the derelictions of the past are of course being neutralized consistently by a deeply imbedded racism that has become metabolized in the blood stream of American society.

Any hopes for urban solutions must face the fact that the increased number of Black people in the cities has served only to intensify problems whose origin began back in the days when the large cities were almost entirely white.

Answers submitted thus far have been counterproductive. Urban renewal plans, translated by many Blacks as "people-removal" plans, have generated new forms of hostility toward the white power structure. Public housing plans have also fallen into disrepute, even those that would "integrate" Black families into white suburban "retreats." Family planning schemes have generated a seething anger among Black youth. And here we should say a word about the Black community's view of population control.

Many Black youth sense a fear on the part of certain scientists, social workers, politicians, and others that the population growth of Black people in America will get out of hand; thus it must be controlled or even reversed. The dubious motives for this concern have never been articulated to the satisfaction of Black critics. Rather, explantions have been submerged in some generalized fears about the inability of this nation's life support system to feed, clothe, house, and otherwise accommodate a sizeable increase in the total population. This seemingly deliberate evasion of a responsibility specifically to cries of alarm from the Black community has tended to give substance to fears that population control really means not only that, but also mind control, controlled wars, and youth control through faulty justice systems in our urban centers—all directed at the gradual and controlled disintegration of the Black community, until it is small enough to be "integrated" or otherwise eliminated.

In other words, an increasing number of Black youth and others believe that population control is another element in a deliberately conceived plan of genocide for Black people. One only needs to visit the Black Topographical Center on Chicago's Southside (open only to Black people) to grasp the intensity of these concerns.

Reading thoughtful discussions of Black concern in such books as, Sam Greenlee's *The Spook Who Sat by the Door* also substantiates the prevalence of views concerning genocide on the part of even many Black intellectual leaders. In his book, *The Man Who Cried I Am*, John Williams describes a scheme called the "King Alfred Plan" for Black population control that some consider the natural corollary of birth control plans for Black people.

Black people are convinced that this country can feed, without any real strain on its resources, a population at least twice as large, while contributing at the same time to the feeding of the rest of the world. Similarly, leaders in shaping Black thought believe that new communities encompassing new styles of life could easily be built in areas that presently are neglected wastelands. So neither food nor space are real problems, especially if the nation can defeat its reluctance to make radical changes in its political and economical structures.

But even accepting arguments favoring population control, the arguments cannot support the conclusion that the growth of the Black population should be controlled. On the contrary, the current nature of things in America speaks very forcefully for a need to hold down white population growth while encouraging Black, red, and brown people to multiply geometrically, without restraints—at least until such time as white Americans feel compelled to practice as well as profess our country's highest ideals. To those who would consider this view synonymous with one encouraging expansion of the poor, the Jesse Jacksons and Ralph Abernathys, Black humanists of the first order, would cry shame. For we could at the same time take actions to redistribute wealth, redefine concepts of universal education, and rebuild our national society as a model for all humanity to emulate.

We have talked about unemployment and attitudes that encourage strife as indices of past practice in America. But the evidence of unconscionable national behavior does not end there. The shortsightedness and neglect of the past are also embarrassingly evident in housing and in educational opportunities, or lack of such, for minorities.

Most of the ill-planned programs to revitalize decaying communities have not worked. Activities in the areas of slum clearance, expressways, public housing, and urban redevelopment, coming too late as it were, have only intensified the very conditions they were designed to remedy. Slum clearance, for example, has only increased overcrowding among the lowest income groups and shifted the slums to new locations. In the meantime segregated neighborhoods continue to assure segregated schools, always inferior. The children in these schools continue to be deprived of equal educational opportunities by a variety of circumstances well detailed in a proliferation of published reports.

The delapidated buildings labeled as schools have become sinks of despair and breeding grounds for narcotics addiction and crimes of violence. Their most efficient function seems to be that of processing Black youth from the community to jails, equally decrepit.

A federal census in 1970 revealed there were 4,037 county and city jails in which 160,863 people were incarcerated. Most of the jails are overcrowded, old, and house a population that is far more Black than white.* In other words, an intimate relationship exists for Black people between the jails and the schools. They not only look alike, but they contribute in similar ways to the dehumanizing of Black youth. Essentially the situation with respect to jails mirrors many of the injustices and evils demonstrated in the rest of U. S. society. The depths of those evils were dramatically exposed at Attica Prison in the fall of 1971.

Of all those held in city and county jails, most had not been

*Black prisoners in Federal penitentiaries are 28 percent of the total prison population compared with the 12 percent Blacks represent in the national population.

TABLE

The figures in this Table represent the number of prisoners being held without conviction in the jails of the nation's cities (1970).

Alabama: 1,597	Nebraska: 327
Alaska: 55	Nevada: 472
Arizona: 887	New Hampshire: 107
Arkansas: 707	New Jersey: 2,604
California: 12,730	New Mexico: 479
Colorado: 980	New York: 8,707
Connecticut: NA	North Carolina: 1,883
Delaware: NA	North Dakota: 94
Florida: 4,734	Ohio: 3,062
Georgia: 2,752	Oklahoma: 1,175
Hawaii: 61	Oregon: 709
Idaho: 237	Pennsylvania: 4,138
Illinois: 3,508	Rhode Island: NA
Indiana: 1,800	South Carolina: 1,031
Iowa: 369	South Dakota: 175
Kansas: 659	Tennessee: 1,773
Kentucky: 1,527	Texas: 7,654
Louisiana: 2,272	Utah: 326
Maine: 82	Vermont: 20
Maryland: 1,976	Virginia: 1,540
Massachusetts: 674	Washington: 1,113
Michigan: 2,716	Washington, D.C.: 933
Minnesota: 487	West Virginia: 530
Mississippi: 865	Wisconsin: 618
Missouri: 1,655	Wyoming: 79
Montana: 200	

NA: Figures not available. Jails are State-operated and not included in this survey.

convicted of any crime. Many prisoners are too poor to put up bail money while waiting for trial, and one of the most common sources of rebellion inside the jail system is the intolerable delay in preferring charges and holding trials.

The cases of Angela Davis and of the thirteen Black Panthers in New York bear dramatic witness to the exploitation of weaknesses in the legal system by the seemingly always present repressive forces acting in the name of justice.

Angela Davis was held without bail, another way of saying there is not enough money in the world to persuade the "prosecution" that the accused was "innocent until proven guilty." The fact that she was held under a law of dubious constitutionality accentuates further the bitter determination of the "justice system" to resist efforts of reform.*

The thirteen Black Panthers were victimized by excessive bonds of up to $100,000 that forced them to spend 25 months in jail before they were found innocent. The jury took 90 minutes to find all thirteen innocent.

The jails and reformatories where so many Black youth pass the years usually spent in school are a national disgrace. Most lack educational and recreational facilities. Most are equipped to do nothing but hold prisoners behind bars for the duration of their sentences. What schooling they do receive is more often than not "schooling" in crime and sexual perversions and brutality.

Of the 3,300 jails in large communities, 85 percent not only have no educational or recreational facilities, but half lack even medical facilities, and one-fourth are without facilities for visitors. Often the mentally disturbed, the hardened criminal, and the confused adolescent are all dumped together, with no effort at segregation according to age or nature of offense, and all this under conditions of severe overcrowding and filth. The definition of the word *dehumanizing* as it applies to the interrelated processes in the schools and jails should now be quite clear.

The penalty for being Black is often oppressive.

Not the least of the many devastating irritants with which Blacks and other neglected minorities are forced to live is housing that demeans and sometimes kills.

In 1970, two-hundred and seventy lead poisoning cases were officially recorded in Washington, D.C. alone. Health officials

*Angela Davis took advantage of this opportunity to make visible other blatant contradictions in the American legal system, thus improving it.

estimate that 10 percent of all children who lived in old housing have too much lead in their bodies. Ten percent of these are so sick they should be hospitalized, even though most are not. The families of most poisoned children don't know they are ill.

The major source of the problem is old houses in the heart of the city. Once the homes of the rich, now they are the only places available to the poor. The rich, of course, wanted the best, so they painted with lead, decades ago. Lead was the finest paint —more opaque, more durable—but after decades of rain on windowsills and slipshod care, the paint is chipping and falling. A few flakes of paint, not more than the size of a thumbnail, are a potentially lethal dose if eaten regularly for a few weeks or months (it varies from child to child). They may be on a baby's bottle, dropped on a littered floor and eventually placed in his own mouth by an unwary child. The situation is cruel, inhumane, and intolerable.

For these and other reasons implicit in this discussion the fabric of American life is threatened as never before. Events of recent years offer convincing evidence that we cannot rely on gradualism in our country any longer as a response to racism and injustice. It must be emphasized again and again that any future racial peace and economic prosperity will depend on our ability to direct the same degree of will to these causes that we directed to the mastery of military technology and manned space flight.

Conditions throughout American society have admittedly not always been this bad. That is why descendents of early immigrants continue in the inane belief that because their folks made it, Blacks only need to try hard in order to achieve similar success. But this is a dangerously naive and narrow view concerning an extremely complex problem rooted in the atavism of slavery and the absurdity of skin color.

In the earliest years of this country's history, things were different for minorities. Newcomers from other lands simply had to learn the ways and skills needed for admission to the American mainstream and they became assimilated into the life of the community. But the color of the non-white, be he Black, red, or brown, has remained in this society an almost insurmountable barrier. Accents can be lost, but color cannot be made to disappear.

The crisis of color has for a long time left no doubt in the minds of most reasonable Americans that this nation is headed for an explosion. But the warnings of recent decades that our country is in trouble have met a leadership that has seen fit to ignore the danger signs in the hope that symptoms of disaster would just disappear. These symptoms haven't, and now the entire nation is in panic over the "urban crisis," "the law and order issue," the "Black problem," and such other issues bearing the popular sociological and political cliches that have become a part of our vocabulary and our way of life.

But no serious approach to relieving the unrest generated by oppressed communities can develop without the primary realization that Black citizens have been justly pressing long neglected grievances.

The indignation erupting in recent years did not occur simply out of a desire for frivolous exercise. Angry youth, whether Black Panthers or Angela Davises, did not curse imaginary obstacles, practices, and procedures. Their resentments were and still are based on insult and denial of their human and civil rights.

There can be no solution to the crisis plaguing the Nation unless there is progress in solving the problems of race. This bugaboo of America, which renders her vulnerable to the attacks of her opponents, is the enigma with which this country must deal. The outlook, however, is not an optimistic one, probably because of the lack of an appropriate ethical response by our most important institutions. Yet, religious prejudice has been considerably mitigated since World War II, resulting from the shock to our sensibilities by the murder of seven million Jews and later the election and assassination of our first Roman Catholic President, the charismatic John F. Kennedy. If Americans are capable of throwing off at least the worst vestiges of religious intolerance, surely we are capable of doing no less with respect to skin color.

If our universities, churches, and other social institutions continue to practice discrimination, however, what can be expected of the individuals who look to these institutions as their guides and mentors? The failure of our institutions to build the required moral base at the level of the individual is probably the greatest failure of our recent history.

Yet, the whole responsibility today cannot be placed on institutions, despite their confused intransigence. Much depends on the individual's own moral code and conscience.

There ought to be many in this country who, while seeing the practices adhered to by institutions, are nevertheless intelligent enough to pursue a moral path and refuse to follow the conventional patterns governing social relationships between people of different races and creeds. In other words, *the problems of cities, as with all of America, will be minimized when individual Americans begin to work for a true justice in which each and every person will be judged or condemned solely on the basis of his or her acts.*

Obviously, America is faced with complex problems, but they are not insoluble ones. But it is still up to individuals—individuals educated in humanism—to accept the challenge and assure the future. Much of the angry rhetoric of today is an overt effort to jolt individual apathy with respect to civil and human rights out of existence and force adherence to the laws of the land that *every* American is entitled to.

Civil rights laws should never have been necessary. Their passage even in the '60s simply added to the laws of man in a society already unheeding and unenforcing both the laws of man and God, and unwilling to cure itself of the sickness of racism. This lack of regard for human rights that have already been endorsed by the Constitution, upheld by the courts, and reiterated by laws upon laws, has encouraged the lack of confidence by Black youth in the integrity of the existing system.

It is impressive that many of the leading minds in America are beginning to conclude that education, and higher education in particular, is the most powerful instrument our society possesses for effecting positive social change. Even more impressive is the growing insistence that education exercise this capability in more creative ways.

Certainly the legitimacy of this new position is well established. The true function of the liberal arts has always been to liberate men. These arts have performed this function in the past by adapting themselves to the problems men have faced. They are capable of performing the same function today.

The whole mentality of our society must undergo constant restructuring stimulated by education. But how do educated men, let alone the uneducated or only trained, bridge existing gaps perpetuated by centuries of fear, separation, misunderstanding, concentration on material wealth and power, and imperialistic design? How do we reshape schools to meet the diverse needs of a modern world and those of individual students, academically, emotionally, and morally? Design rather than chance seems the only likely way to begin at this time. Our past tendency to rely on chance for solutions to our problems has only encouraged disaster. Hopes for change based primarily on exigencies of time have usually been nurtured by the lack of initiative and the abundance of the kind of inertia inherent in existing bureaucratic and social structures. Consequently, it is imperative for the future that legislators, businessmen, civic leaders, educators, and scientists—social, physical, and biological—support the need to quit talking about "the problem" and instead begin to engage systematically in carefully planning "the solution." Moreover, all so engaged should realize that the impact on nature *and* society must be calculated with care.

Above all, educators must begin immediately the construction of new modules for maximizing development of each individual human's potential for growth in an optimally conducive life environment. New educational formats must be based on renewed concepts of morality as well as on more accurate insights concerning how people learn, variations in learning styles, the nature of intelligence, motivation and its critical determinants, the effects of environment on intelligence and general health, and the need to remove the social and physical pollutants that destroy the potential of humans and nature alike.

Emphasis in future programs of human development must be

on utilizing the entire environment to help each individual live a full and complete life. New institutions must be built, old ones must be rebuilt. The entire environment must become the classroom of the future; all of it incorporating enlightened concepts of mass human development in the true sense of the word; all of it permeated with the qualities that will facilitate the process of teaching people how to live, love, and enjoy life, together. In this way such terms as morality, democracy, justice, law and order, work and leisure, welfare and service can be redefined and intertwined for the purpose of creating a more perfect society.

Decisions concerning change must always evolve out of a concern for individual self-worth, individual rights, human dignity, economic security, personal independence, and a desire for a better society. The shattered faith of Black, red, brown, and yellow minorities must be restored by decisions and plans for change that reflect honest sincerity and place human values above all else.

Restoration of lost faith demands sincere efforts to strengthen Black and other minority communities and to draw upon them more vigorously for the support the entire nation so urgently needs.

No renewal of faith is possible, of course, if the nation continues to have disordered priorities which see exploration of space as being more important than solutions for racism, poverty, hunger, and inadequate educational programs. Neither will renewed faith, new harmony among people, or preservation of nature's ability to restore itself be achieved by continuing to permit the natural environment to be contaminated in ways which maim and kill.

Direct intervention programs for minority group children and youth must be introduced at an early age, if the nation's shame is to be erased. Only in this way can lessons of freedom, justice, equality, and respect for human dignity be actualized for all citizens.

Our entire citizenry must become sensitive, not only to the degrading psychological consequences of discrimination for Black children, but also to its insidious effects on white children and subsequently the entire society. All must realize, for example, that when white children are taught, directly or otherwise, that they must avoid Black children, they are really being taught that they must be afraid of them. This kind of fear produces hate in addition to feelings of alienation. In consequence, even before adulthood, both white and Black Americans know fear, apprehension, and uncertainty in their orientation toward one another as one result of discriminatory practices in our society.

We have tarried too long. To delay further is to guarantee our destruction as a dignified nation of free people. Theories of gradualism leading to conditions of "too little, too late" must be abandoned. There must be a revolution in this country—a violent revolution, but hopefully not the kind of revolution that is marked by bloodshed and loss of life. That kind of revolution results when no other kind is permitted to evolve. We should welcome, however, a revolution that so jolts the lethargic apathy of this country's basic institutions—especially education—that a return to the status quo is never again possible.

Further, this is a country where the word "revolution" ought to be an honorable one rather than a cause for apprehension and fear. If we cannot adjust to the idea of radical internal change, suddenly initiated, and abruptly implemented, how can there ever be hope for a more peaceful domestic or international environment?

To motivate the change that some know as the requisite of survival, we must recognize the compelling urgency of solving the proliferating crises of our time. We must also recognize the indices of success. It has been said "A house divided cannot stand." But the four cornerstones of the unity we are bound to seek are equality, justice, liberty, and full opportunity for all. Without any one of these, there can be no freedom from the fears plaguing us today—eventually there will be no house to divide.

It isn't very practical, however, to talk about harmonious human interrelationships when a serious imbalance continues to

exist in the power and economic relationships between the
"haves" and the "have-nots." With racism imposing a ceiling on
the upward thrust potential of have-not-minorities, there is little
likelihood of any real gains by them. Economic opportunity and
educational opportunity are intimately related in contemporary
America. Both are essential to the acquisition of power. Without adequate financial support, a community cannot thrive.
Without educational opportunity, economic equality remains a
myth for any aspiring group.

For the nation's very survival as a representative democracy,
political and business leaders must take more significant actions
to eliminate discriminatory employment practices and straighten
out the skewed opportunity structure that limits the upward mobility of so many minority-group Americans.

Lerone Bennett shows penetrating insights through a discussion appearing in the special edition of *Ebony* on "Separation?
Integration? Liberation?—Which Way Black America?"

Bennett writes that peaceful co-existence of white America
and Black America ". . . requires a recognition that the race
problem cannot be solved without profound structural modifi-
cations in 'America,' without real changes in the tax structure
and the relations between the private and public sectors, without
a redefinition of all values and a redistribution of income and
power."

Those concerned with improved moral leadership will also appreciate another statement made in the same article: "Before
Blacks can integrate with whites they must integrate with themselves. . . . Black unity . . . requires Black organization. . . . We
need Black-oriented . . . youth camps, youth centers, colleges,
social welfare organizations, study groups, unions, and political
parties."

Solutions to natural problems created by racism cannot be
achieved in purely idealistic terms. A philosophy of liberation
must evolve out of careful planning accompanied by a frank ap-
praisal of institutions and policies penetrated most deeply by
racism.

One of the basic requisites for a truly pluralistic society, where justice reigns for all, is the elimination of racism from all institutions, but especially from education, the institution which shapes, controls, and directs the lives of so many people in America. Only then can we envision a time when brotherhood is a reality rather than a term of convenience.

3

INSTITUTIONAL RACISM

Racism so permeates the historical legacy of contemporary America that none of our policies and institutions is immune from attack from some quarter for being racist. Yet many people of all races are continually surprised at the mounting evidence of racism in our most prestigious institutions, including education.

They do not seem to understand, further, that institutional racism is not necessarily involved with the racial prejudices of a particular citizen but must be judged by the de facto impact of a policy on the welfare of a minority group. Even the United States Congress has not been immune. The successful political decapitation of Adam Clayton Powell may be the best example. But in more subtle ways this august body has contributed unceasingly since reconstruction to legitimizing racism and perpetuating racial tensions.

The most dramatic political incident involving overt racism, individual and institutional combined, occurred in the state capitol of Georgia where Julian Bond, a youthful Black politician, was denied his seat as an elected representative allegedly because of statements he made in the cause of international peace and Black liberation. Even the eventual intervention of the U.S. Supreme Court could not wipe out this additional blot on the national conscience and on the reputation of the State of Georgia.

The case of Muhammed Ali is another one in point. Although countless public figures, fighters, actors, and others over the past 100 years changed their names at will, the same action by Muhammed Ali in discarding the name Cassius Clay engendered only venom, contempt, and a shower of invective. Even some newspapers refuse to call him by his preferred name for reasons that are inconsistent with their own supposedly established policies. The greatest injustice to this man, however, was the relentless persecution growing out of his refusal to serve in the armed forces. Despite the fact that the basis for refusal was his religious beliefs, he was convicted of draft evasion. The court action precipitated a series of vindictive responses that stripped him of his title and deprived him for over two years of his right to earn a living, even though at the time his case was under legitimate appeal. His eventual vindication by the U.S. Supreme Court sustained the rightness of Muhammed Ali's contention but did not compensate him for months of lost income.

The persecution of the Black Panther Party is still another example. Massive attacks against chapter after chapter, all across the nation, gave support to the suspicion that a calculated plan of elimination was in effect. While other groups, far more destructive in their impact, but predominately white, were being given casual attention at best, Panther Party members were being assassinated in their homes, besieged in their headquarters, and arrested on an almost infinite number of charges.*

*The notorious Fred Hampton case is still embarrassing Chicago's legal authorities. Hampton and a fellow Panther, Mark Clark, died in a raid by a picked police team, and the blatantly inaccurate reports made of that raid placed full responsibility on the Panthers. A Grand Jury investigation seeking an indictment against the state's prosecutor was suppressed until higher court action forced its release, and this investigation implied unrestrained and irresponsible action by the police. An indictment was eventually secured against the State's Attorney and a number of police officers.

The very jails too have become symbols of racial as well as so-cial injustice because of the unjust imprisonment for countless numbers of Black youth. The case of Angela Davis further illus-trates the point, particularly when juxtaposed with the case of Lt. William Calley, convicted by a military court of murdering innocent children, women ,and old men in Vietnam.

Too many victimized Black youth are not convicted criminals; they are suspects being held for trial who cannot make bail. A system which favors the more affluent white youth can only be viewed as institutionalized racism.

Even under European codes which presume guilt and require proof of innocence, a person cannot legally be held indefinitely without any test. Anglo-Saxon law developed the procedure of habeas corpus precisely to stop the practice of locking people away without giving them a chance to answer charges.

The American judicial system, with its requirement of pre-suming innocence until guilt has been proven, unfortunately and unnecessarily has not lived up to its promise. People are put away for long periods without trial, not for lack of good judicial intentions and constitutional guarantees, but because there is a break-down in the justice system as it relates to Black and many other minority youth.

There are many despicable things which young Black men are obliged to endure while unjustly imprisoned. Overcrowding of jails has reached the point where more than twice as many youths as the building was meant to hold are jammed into cells that are often rat-infested. This condition stems in part from paralysis of the courts, so blocked and disorganized that some people are kept waiting as long as two years for trial. It is also a result of the tendency of some police officers to become both judge and jury. It represents another form of "police brutality."

Middle-class prisoners—the embezzler, the gambler, the tax evader, the drunken driver, the shoplifter—can raise bail and go on living normally until his or her day in court. But as indicated earlier, the minority-group youth seldom has the financial re-sources to do likewise.

One immediate concern among Blacks, shared by many city

officials during the volatile summer months of recent years, is the inadequacy of funds to solve the problems of urban youths. Most see traditional and entrenched American racism, detailed in 1969 in the report by the President's Commission on Civil Disorders, as a continuing deterrent to Black progress. And many are disturbed by new expressions of anti-Black bias from working-class whites as Black people have attempted to compete more and more with whites for jobs.

Generally, Blacks admit to being encouraged by the national Black successes, like the election of a Black mayor in Newark, but this is often more than counterbalanced in their minds by increases in "justifiable homicides" of Blacks by police all over the country.

Blacks are also despondent about the consistent unemployment of Black youth and are convinced that the "southern strategies" of presidential candidates work to the detriment of Black Americans because these seek to expand the political party in and around the white South, and among white, conservative middle-class Americans elsewhere.

In the South, white hostilities toward Blacks have now taken on the more polite and smiling subtleties of the North.

Black frustrations are more kinetically explosive today in the South and the North, the result of white resistance, because more and more Blacks are becoming aware that repressions of freedom need not continue and they are putting forth efforts to stop them. And the rising Black frustrations, across the nation, can still be seen in the areas that have for many decades been focal points in the Black struggle—police conduct, unemployment, housing (new urban renewal), and education.

Still another area of Black frustration is that of official promises—either stated promises to prevent riots or implied promises like a war on poverty. The frustration is imminent when none of the promises is kept or all are broken.

One of the more volatile Black-white conflicts continues to be the day-to-day relationship between the basically white-dominated police department and the urban, Black, poor citizen.

It must be realized that most of the urban disorders of recent years started with police-citizen confrontations.

"Generally, white policemen feel they are better than Blacks and they take the attitude that it's 'either them or us,'" said Renault Robinson, the Chicago patrolman who helped organize the Afro–American Patrolmen's League. The league was formed, said Mr. Robinson, to counter "within the system" both the physical and verbal brutalization of Blacks and the poor by law officers.

"A citizen in an affluent neighborhood will always get a 'sir' from a Chicago policeman but the policeman will be mostly hostile in a Black, Spanish-speaking or hillbilly neighborhood," the officer said.

Black youths are now demanding Black policemen in their neighborhoods who know the community. When asked why, a typical answer might be: "He don't call me 'nigger' when he arrests me; don't call me 'boy' when he gives me a ticket; don't go through a whole lot of changes when I'm in a car with a light-skinned Black woman."

A prominent criminologist, Professor Thomas Todd, former U.S. Attorney and Professor of Law at Northwestern University, added, "Statistics show clearly that Black people in America are still more likely to be arrested, found guilty, and sentenced than are whites." And Judge George Crockett of Detroit's Recorders Court maintains that while "the public likes to believe that the courts are crystallized in a majestic neutrality, the truth is that they are not. They would certainly not allow the beating of any prisoner, 'Black or white,' where they live but they reflect an easy tolerance of police brutality in districts where they work."

Racism, as it exists in America, is without a doubt a major foundation for all of its problems—in its schools as well as its courts and elsewhere.

Compounding the negative influences of racism, of course, is the immense impact of automation. But the most significant factor in the continued failure of Black America is America's enterprises dominated by white leadership.

While individual racism consists of overt acts by individuals, institutional racism is less overt, far more subtle, and less identifiable in terms of the acts committed. Hence, racism involves much more than discrimination against Black people by white people.

Racism grew initially out of rationalizations to justify a simple economic fact: that the colonies needed labor and resorted to Negro labor because it was cheapest and best. It continues for similar and for even more vicious reasons. It is now so permeating that it actually becomes a part of the fabric of this society. It gets intimately involved in how people feel about themselves, other people, the institutions of which they are a part, and the entire world in which they live. In fact, racism shapes how people look at the world. At the same time racist behavior persists on a day-to-day basis—in the name of the law, in the name of mutual respect, in the name of charity, etc. It is a system that goes on day in and day out: one which gives most white people certain kinds of privileges and denies those same rights to most non-white people.

Before a society can become nonracist, it must recognize it is racist. The indices of racism must be identified and analyzed critically in terms of causes and effects. The basis may then be formulated for a philosophy of liberation, conceived out of the ethnic and racial unity required for any hope of ultimate success.

Paulo Freire comments on this phenomenon: "[T]o overcome . . . oppression . . . requires a critical recognition of its course, so that through transforming action another situation can be created—one which makes possible the pursuit of *being more fully human*. When one initiates an authentic struggle to create the new situation which will be born with the overcoming of the old, one is already fighting to be more fully human."

The courage to attempt new programs, to eradicate racism, and to encourage acceptance and appreciation of all individuals as human beings must come from the leadership of education, business, industry, as well as the Federal Government, or else tension and hostility will destroy any possibility of peaceful racial and class interactions.

One thing should be clear above all others, middle-class whites are not going to experience any peace as they traverse a city slum to get to air-conditioned offices until a more balanced economy and a just system of life prevails for all.

Without educational opportunity, economic equality will remain a myth for an aspiring group. It should be elementary also that racial harmony requires equality of economic opportunity as a forerunner. Fallacies in previous efforts to cope with racial and ethnic conflict included lack of a serious effort to introduce economic equity as a precondition. It should have been no surprise therefore that the civil rights movement died an ignominious death. The last flicker of hope for racial harmony under the old set of presumptions died when an assassin's bullet ended the life of the Rev. Dr. Martin Luther King.

Now a new set of presumptions obtains. Among these is the understanding that unless racism is eliminated from all aspects of life in America, and economic equity is established, no real progress will occur in the human relations climate of this country.

Political, educational, and business leaders must, therefore, take some significant actions to eliminate discriminatory practices and straighten out the skewed opportunity structure that limits the upward mobility of so many minority-group Americans.

The reaction of Black people to years of frustrated attempts to gain equality should have been predictable. Black people are saying today that they do not want to integrate into a racist society. They are now aware that many integration programs have ended up as new support for notions of white supremacy. The plain fact is, they assert, that nothing truly significant has happened to confront the issue of racism: "Our last chance resides in our ability to solve our own problems."

Preston Wilcox, the Black educator, contends that elimination of racism from all institutions is an imperative factor in the hope of Black people for a better life. Using education as an example, he refers to the need for a humanistic-liberal approach, in which emphasis will switch from teaching to learning, and where the school will be transformed from a building for the one-way transmission of information into a center for inquiry.

He stresses that the only way to create a humane society is to create and maintain institutions that are themselves humane.

To cope successfully with deeply imbedded, though subtle, racist practices there must be a moral purpose underlying the existence of all institutions. Vague ideas about morality must be converted into meaningful moral ideas that can be internalized by the institution and the individuals comprising its staff.

The ramifying implications of these principles are far reaching as a basis for viewing education as a liberating force.

Essentially, there must be the recognition that all people must be encouraged to acquire the skills to humanize their existence, to protect their right to be whom they need to be, and to experience the beauty of living.

Positive values must be primary concerns in educating people, and we must understand that any failure to educate people for humanism is to guarantee their ultimate destruction. Failure to support this latter principle creates programs that educate people to participate in the destruction of their own identities and cultures, turn them against each other, and substitute alien values for their own.

A variety of Black educators have developed some important corollaries to these fundamental principles of humanitarianism. The society as a whole must come to understand that all Black children and youth are human and educable. Further, education for Black people must be viewed as a rehumanization and decolonialization process. Black youth must be taught that they hold in common African descendancy and victimization by racism. All youth must be taught a respect for native cultural differences, a resistance to all forms of oppression, and recognition of their responsibility to defend their right to become whom they want to become as long as the expression of that right does not demand the oppression of others. They must be made aware that to condone racism is to participate in their own destruction and that of their own people. And above all they must know that they have a right and an obligation to define themselves and the terms by which they will relate to others.

Education must become a process that educates for this kind

of liberation and for joyful human survival, nothing less. In essence, the principles cited mean that education which effectively
overlooks the aspirations and the survival requirements of the
masses of people is irrelevant and immoral.

The education of Black people and all others among the poor
and oppressed must free them from psychological dependence on
others and teach them to think and act on their own. It must
also provide students an opportunity to select out, design, and
articulate their own values and to discern the impact of these
values on their behavior, their attitudes, and their relationships
with others.

The abilities required for self-liberation as discussed here do
not reside solely in intellectual talents but in the psychological
and emotional ability to rid one's self of a need to be directed
(controlled) by others as well. Essential constructs for Black
people in their efforts to achieve humanistic goals through education include the need to forget their *isolation* from white people (integration, separation, assimilation, etc.) and deal with their
alienation from each other. They must replace any *need to integrate into* white communities with a sense of urgency about
developing their own communities. This attitude supports no
particular position concerning separatism, pluralism, or even integration. It just recognizes reality.

Whitney Young stated shortly before his death in 1971:

> Black people have been here for more than 400 years. We
> have contributed dearly in all the gains this land has made and
> suffered disproportionately in all its failures. We are already
> segregated for the most part.
> . . . [but] white Americans who engage in wishful-thinking
> that we are going to take them off the hook and solve their prob-
> lems by . . . collectively moving to separate states or leaving
> en masse for Africa should be told loudly and clearly: forget it;
> we are here to stay and in the process we are either going to
> make this country live up to its Judeo-Christian ethic and its
> democratic promise, or see it go down the drain of history as im-
> moral and hypocritical, deserving of its fate.

Separatism of the races is without a doubt a reality forced for
the time being upon the Black masses and other selected minori-

ties by a recalcitrant white majority. It should not be surprising, therefore, that after long years of struggling and shedding blood for the dream of full integration into the American mainstream Black Americans have now shifted gears and have decided that Black is beautiful and Black communities can be beautiful communities, economically, physically, and in human interrelationships.

Amazingly, when Black America announced intentions to struggle for control and beautification of their own communities, while striving for optimal self-sufficiency in all their affairs, the white community recoiled. It was as if the Black community had demanded for itself all these years degrading slums, inferior schools, poor economic opportunity, and generally fourth-class citizenship. The white community actually cried out with indignant piety against what they called Black separatism, while still refusing to integrate the ghettos themselves or to build housing projects in their own suburban retreats. Because those who control housing and financing will it, segregation continues today and separation becomes more firmly imbedded as a way of life in America. Many in Black America have now decided to accommodate to their condition, at least temporarily.

Those who deny the deliberate attempts of official white America to maintain separation of races as a way of life are exposing a dangerous naivete. An astonishing amount of political ingenuity by white politicians, northern and southern, has gone into attempts to perpetuate segregation, or avoid integration. New York outlawed busing and then devised a decentralized school system for New York City, which is being fought in the courts. In Chicago, politicians managed to stop busing plans, and came up with a plan for integrating teachers that is an insult to the Black community. Los Angeles was ordered by a judge to integrate its schools, a move which would require massive busing. Suddenly the State Assembly passed an anti-busing bill, and the legislature began working on a plan to split the city's school district into 24 parts. The judge was voted out of office the following year.

Instead of providing better support systems for schools attempting to make integration work, political leaders tolerate trimmed budgets and allow propagation of the belief that racial hostility, rather than political and social ambivalence are the real problems. The indecisive leadership of President Nixon on such as the busing issue and the demagogic racist behavior of George Wallace did nothing to defuse the volatile situation.

Oddly enough the "separate but equal" doctrine which was never achieved when it was the law of the land, has now become a determined goal for many of the disappointed, the disillusioned and the betrayed Black people.

The Southern Regional Council issued a special report in 1968 entitled: *Lawlessness and Disorder: Fourteen Years of Failure in Southern School Desegregation.* That report discussed how many Black parents and students, reflecting in varying degrees a concept of "Black awareness," are expressing the belief that school desegregation is no longer a relevant issue.

Many Black students are now crying, the report states, "Why don't whites ever transfer to our schools? Why should we be the ones to do all the sacrificing?" The same attitude was expressed by their parents with the insistence that "quality education" must be achieved for all and that their children should not always be the ones to suffer the pain, the estrangement, and the cruelty inherent in desegregating a school.

The Council also produced a report entitled, *Voices from the South: Black Students Talk about Their Experiences in Desegregated Schools.* On the basis of what these Black youth said, the Council concluded: "What seems most evident is that Black youth in the South will no longer play a passive role in decisions affecting their lives and futures."

The report by the Council referred to U. S. Justice Department figures which showed that more than 50 percent of the South's Black students were enrolled in schools with whites in 1970. The experience was documented as traumatic for both, principally because only the rooms in predominantly white schools were integrated, not the students. Moreover, Black professional educators were demoted and dismissed by the thousands.

Testimony by various witnesses before the Senate Select Committee on Equal Educational Opportunity in 1970 revealed that "books, microscopes, desks, and even whole school buildings disappeared from Southern schools only to reappear in new, all-white segregated academies." One North Carolina district turned over public school buildings to new, segregated private schools for one dollar a year. These new forms of hypocrisy validate the appropriateness of apprehensions about the inadequacies of integration efforts and certify that they are dishonest in most respects.

The principal reason for school integration difficulties may result because white school boards with unreconstructed views still control the so-called desegregated schools. This condition has been termed the main reason why in one Mississippi school 55 percent of the Black teachers were fired. Percentages ranging from 23 to 40 percent were fired in nine other Mississippi schools.

Other hypocritical practices at "integrated" schools include separate class rooms, separate lunch and gym periods, and even separate bells so that Blacks and whites do not use the hall together.

In one Louisiana parish, buses pick up Blacks at 5:30 a.m. so that whites can ride separately at a more sensible hour. Afro haircuts and dress are banned in many schools (north and south) and participation of Black students in many school activities is deliberately limited.

All of this resistance to the "law of the land" has had enormous impact on the Black community's attitudes toward integration that was a primary goal for virtually all Blacks until a few years ago.

To Blacks and all other minorities, quality education, integrated or otherwise, is literally the basis of life, liberty, and the pursuit of happiness in this society. From this fact springs the serious probability of increasing violence if that kind of education is denied. Such violence might work to the temporary advantage of a politician or a sector, but in the long run it can only work to the disadvantage of the country.

Fundamentally and alarmingly, racism in education may be

even more widespread in more parts of the North than it is south of the Mason–Dixon line. A study by the Department of Health, Education and Welfare showed that 61 percent of all Black students in the northern U. S. still attended schools that were 96 percent or more Black.

Of all non-southern school systems, none is more segregated than that of the nation's capital. Whites have virtually abandoned Washington's public schools, and, as a result, 89 percent of the Black children go to school largely with other Blacks. The situation is little different in other large cities in the North.

If integration had moved ". . . with all deliberate speed," as mandated by the Supreme Court, thereby permitting the Black American a full and immediate opportunity to develop self-esteem and to retain his basic cultural identity, the now impressive move toward building beautiful and powerful Black communities, replete with institutions controlled by Black people, probably would not have arisen. But the message consistently received by the Black American was one of deceit.

The Black American has with good reason come to interpret integration to mean ultimately the disintegration or the disappearance of his race and culture.

The Black movement today strenuously seeks not only to preserve the basic identity of the Black American but, more importantly, to foster the development of a different image, one which will erase the previous negative image ascribed to him. Integration is not necessary to the achievement of these objectives. Elimination of racism is.

Most Black people today, considering integration as irrelevant, see the task as one of uniting Black people to build decent Black institutions in Black communities and to create equal opportunity for Black people in the economic mainstream.

The only road left for the Black man is community building —building his own, that is. Although many in the white community express doubt that the Black man in America has the capacity to create a genuine community with organs for cooperation and self-help, this is not true. Black people have already developed some objects of identification for Black people every-

where. And most realize that it must be a do-it-yourself job if
anything lasting is to be done for the betterment of the Black
community. The schools must become the cornerstone of that
effort.

The Black student quite properly views the school of today—
north or south, integrated or segregated—as an integral part of
his insoluble problems. He is presented a curriculum which is
geared neither to his interests nor his experiences. He is given
tests that demean him and certify his inferiority. From the time
the student enters kindergarten until he reaches college, and
often beyond, he is subjected to a succession of examinations
whose practical function it is to sort and classify him for the
convenience of teachers and administrators. There is perhaps no
more pervasive influence in American education than the standardized tests of "mental ability" and "accomplishment." These
tests play a major role in determining what doors in life will be
open to Black youth.

The content of the examinations and the educational values
and priorities reflected by them tend to become those adopted
by the school. Because the tests constitute education's primary
common standard of performance, they shape in large measure
what is to be taught and how.

The pinnacle of the examination system is the testing program
administered by the College Entrance Examination Board to
two million high school students each year. So, when the College
Board's Commission on Tests in the summer of 1970 pronounced
the board's tests "insensitive, narrowly conceived and inimical to
the interests of many youths," it was rendering a judgment on
American education itself, and on one of the major mechanisms
through which American society has incorrectly determined intellectual potential and wrongly conferred opportunity and status.

In calling for extensive reform of the College Board testing
program, the Commission said that the program had focused on
the rather specialized needs of educational institutions, while
failing to serve the diverse interests of minority students. Like
most other standardized tests at all levels of schooling, including
so-called intelligence tests, the College Board examinations as-

sess qualities essentially rooted in the ability to speak, read, and write standard English and to handle quantitative, or mathematical concepts.

The Commission admitted, as a revolutionary first, that there was much more to mental excellence than verbal and mathematical ability; hence the College Board examinations penalize countless minority youth who do not fit the standard, traditional, somewhat specialized academic mold.

The Commission urged that the College Board examinations be reconstituted so they assess not only verbal and quantitative facility, but also such dimensions of excellence as musical and artistic talent; sensitivity and commitment to social responsibility; political and social leadership; political, vocational, technical, and mechanical skills; style of analysis and synthesis; ability to express one's self through oral, nonverbal, or graphic means; ability to organize and manage information; ability to adapt to new situations; characteristics of temperament, and work habits under varying conditions of demand. This is one example of an initial stride toward deinstitutionalizing racism. There are not many others.

Recasting of attitudes on tests may open the doors of opportunity to many who now find them closed and may also force many schools and colleges to recast their instructional programs to serve more adequately the talents and interests of the minority group student. The change of attitude may also give some "symmetry" to a system now heavily weighted against Black and other minority people.

Many educators, especially Black ones, have long known that tests cannot measure native or inherited ability, particularly when they do not allow for differences in life styles among those taking the tests. The earlier acceptance of test validity was simply a way of accepting at the same time the idea of limited educability for Black, brown, and red people.

The so-called "test experts" of early days did not argue that human differences do not exist, but rather that in America *lower class* and *race* always coincide with the judgments of the tests that determine the organization of American education. It was thus inevitable that psychologists in American education would develop a testing "science" that paid little attention to the "science" of human potential and how people learn. Tests, as currently constituted, really only measure the effects of racist treatment on Black youth.

For many years the myth was perpetuated by various standardized tests that Black children are poor in their expression of verbal style. Black verbal style *does* differ from the white verbal style. This difference means only, however, that the Black experience produces unique verbal skills found mainly in the Black community and that these skills are not validated or accepted in the middle-class oriented classroom. Many Black children play a game called the "dozens" and play it rather well. The "dozens" simply refers to a game of verbal insult in reference to another's parents. This writer has known Black youth who were masters at this game which requires verbal adroitness and high fluency. These same youth did not read well and did not enjoy school, despite their ability to phrase their "dozens" in "iambic pentameters" with ease, and create an emotional stir in their listeners.

The ability of most Blacks to "rap" (engage in face-to-face discussion) is well established. Strangely, this skill carries little weight in most educational programs as now constituted.

These facts point up why two common threads run through all of the unrest observed today among Black youth. The first is a violent reaction to deception in any form. The second involves their belief in the need for a new form of humanism. They express themselves in this area through a desire to transform all existing institutions so that they clearly and directly serve to improve the quality of human life for all people.

It should be easy to understand in the face of prevailing circumstances why Blacks want to control their own communities and to manage their own institutions—not because they are isolationists or racists, but because of their frustration resulting from white resistance to creation of a truly humanized society of people living in an environment of justice and equality.

In essence, they are saying that the only method of assuring

that the present intractability will change is through a willingness on the part of Black people, themselves, to pay the price of
freedom and lead the way to a new humanism for all Americans.
Results of the past make the future seem unpromising in terms
of achieving this noble ideal.

Where then does the hope for the future lie? The answer,
very simple, though highly complex in its application, is based
in a more willing responsiveness and a greater sensitivity by all
Americans.

With respect to education, a new set of structural relationships must exist among teachers, administrators, students, parents, and community representatives. School personnel must
come to view all of the other components mentioned in new
ways. Improved procedures for relating to one another will help
school communities to become communities of equals, all having in the main common concerns, and serving as a basis for a
broader unity inside and outside the classroom.

To give substance to their desire for freedom from racism,
most now feel that Black people must achieve political and economic power—the kind of raw, audacious, naked power that will
create the countervailing force needed to force negotiation. But
they also realize that power, like freedom, is not easily gained, because those who have it do not want to give it up and will not
do so easily.

For Blacks to achieve the power that will guarantee their ultimate freedom, as U.S. Representative John Conyers has said so
often, there are some things they must be willing to do, a price
they must be willing to pay.

The major beginning involves what Congressman Ron Del-
lums has called a determination to develop a model of Black
unity. But the vitality and depth of creative Black unity can be
realized only if the Black community is freed from the corroding
effects of hostile influences. Paramount among these influences,
of course, is the present system of education which must be
changed into a tool of liberation.

The current condition must be altered so that an educational
system will derive which contributes to and reflects the vitality

of the Black experience. The new system must be relevant and responsive to the needs of Black people and to threats to their physical survival. It must also be a system that supports Black survival in the broadest cultural terms.

The system being sought must promote the self-determined growth of the Black community, liberate the minds and souls of Black people, and mobilize Black resources for the development of meaningful human values and institutions that humanize rather than destroy human potential. The new system must at the same time help the white community come to more than a superficial understanding of the events involving great Black leaders, significant Black movements, and the presence of racism in every aspect of American life.

The white liberals who bled and fought for voter registration in the South, for integration in the schools and colleges, for the end of discrimination in hiring practices, and the end of discrimination elsewhere in our society need not be discouraged by this newly emerging attitude of self-sufficiency among Black people. They are still needed, but in new roles in their *own* communities.

The vast majority of Blacks continue to believe there is room in this country for all of us to find a good life. What they are saying is nothing more nor less than this: We demand the same rights and privileges as white Americans.

Self-sufficiency and self-determination will help bring Blacks and whites together in eventual harmony. All of our children have a right to this legacy and we have a responsibility to see that they get it.

The Black baby born in America today, regardless of the section or the state in which he is born, has about one-half as much chance of completing high school as a white baby born in the same place, on the same day; one-third as much chance of completing college; one fourth as much chance of becoming employed; about one-seventh as much chance of earning $10,000 a year; a life expectancy which is seven years shorter, and the prospects of earning only half as much.

John F. Kennedy

4

CREATIVE RESPONSE TO CRISIS

The environment in which today's children are growing up is not the humane world that we could create. Policies and programs exist that make the environment less than the liberating framework for human creativity and satisfaction that it ought to be. The leaders of America can and should create an environment fit for children to grow in, one in which adults can take pride. Leadership of the past has been sadly deficient in this respect. The future must surely be different.

Those attempting to build and reshape Black communities and such institutions as education are coming to understand that the future of all of America and the future of Black Americans will be determined by the quality of leadership that education can help to build. Black potential for leadership must not be overlooked in the process.

Leadership of the past from the Black community, though there has not been enough of it, has been inspiring through its willingness to put honor above all things and to view freedom as the most precious of all human rights. History has documented the leadership of Crispus Attucks of Boston, who integrated the first revolution in America and left his blood stained indelibly in the ground of this land; Denmark Vesey, a freedman who made it known that no Black man of honor could enjoy freedom while his brothers and sisters suffered as slaves; Nat Turner, who laid to rest forever the myth that Black people could ever accept their status as subhumans in America.

In later years, there was Frederick Douglass, another freedom fighter without parallel; and still later W. E. B. Dubois, an intellectual giant who lived two life times in one; Marcus Garvey, Martin Luther King, and Malcolm X. The beat—the freedom beat—has gone on, developed out of the irrepressible vigor of the Black community into the kind of leadership that could revitalize this nation and save it from itself.

Unfortunately, a new kind of barrier has developed for Black students aspiring to leadership in contemporary life. Even more serious and divisive than the generation gap or the socioeconomic gap is the chasm between Black young people today and their teachers who function as if we were still in the era of Mark Twain.

In many predominantly Black schools, there is continuing reliance on the teacher-centered classroom and written and printed words, while most audiovisual equipment and materials are relegated to a far corner in a storage closet. Few teachers in these schools are prepared to work with the Black student of the 1970s with the tools available to them. This lack of competence can no longer be tolerated. Emphasis must shift from defensive didactics to multiple-modality, learner-centered approaches, sensitive to the ways in which the student learns most easily and using all the resources available to the contemporary educator. There is also need for some emotional retooling of most teachers and some new insights concerning learning styles and human potential.

Educators earnestly concerned with creating new avenues of opportunity for Black youth through education must also become reconciled to some bitter realities. The ravages of years of injustice are starkly visible through the behavior of young Blacks who are on the verge of giving up on the nation and its educational system. Frustration and disappointment will be the primary rewards for the naive missionary-type teacher who today expects to find much evidence of love of country or respect for the flag among Black youth. Typically, many Black youth refuse to stand when the national anthem is played, turn their backs when the flag is displayed, and scoff at the notion of the United States of America as a symbol of freedom, equality, and justice. With good reason they see all authority figures as symbols of the oppression they have been forced to endure all of their lives. These are symbols to be hated, feared, and fought.

It really makes no difference whether the authority figure is a policeman, school principal, teacher, welfare worker, agency head, or politician. Incumbents in such positions are distrusted and subject to confrontation. In fact, the *easiest* way for the Black youth to approach any of these is through confrontation paradigms of one kind or another. Moreover, since he is constantly reacting to implied or actual intimidations from oppressive authority in his environment, the only countervailing force he can conceive to be potentially effective is his own kind of intimidation.

Education has often been viewed as the one remaining institution with the moral integrity to grapple with the social injustices victimizing Blacks and other minority youth. Time after time educational opportunity has been represented to Black youth as the passport to freedom; yet when these youth seek entry to this land of opportunity the border is closed to them. Or still worse, they are sold a counterfeit ticket allowing them in but filled with unfair conditions from which they have no recourse.

Thus the major problem of education for the Black community is clearly not economic alone, but philosophic as well. The unfairness prevailing in most compensatory education programs, for example, makes them hypocritical. Their failure cannot be rationalized away. Neither can the failure of school administrators to provide an adequate system of supportive service and a positive environment after making special effort to recruit Black students be explained away in acceptable terms.

Learning habits are formed by the life style of the community in which the individual resides during formative years. They are acquired slowly over time. And they are most difficult, if not impossible, to apply when the learning environment is alien, unstable, uncertain, and hostile to the student.

The need of the Black community to control its own educational system is also a part of the total crisis. This general problem can only be met through expanded control within their own community of the educational resources available to Black students.

Decentralization of power, effected from above, has been widely discussed as a possible answer to prevailing insensitivities. So far, it has proved a decisive political failure in New York and it may be some time before the experiment of community control can gain any real momentum. Even in Chicago, the "successful" Woodlawn experiment in community control of a small group of schools ended without bringing on any meaningful change in the archaic structure of Chicago's public schools. Yet the issue of community control must not be permitted to expire without more effort.

Admittedly the problems of decentralizing school control render the entire question complex. Primary among the problems, however, is a characteristic lethargy compounded by partisan politics. As cities have proliferated in size, crises and problems have expanded, yet power over the schools has tended to become concentrated in the hands of a smaller and smaller percentage of the community. In most school systems board members are either appointed politically, or elected under circumstances controlled by the traditional two-party system. A board member is then responsive either to the appointing authority or to the political party he feels is responsible for his election instead of to the welfare of students.

Excluded for the most part have been the voices of Black parents in the various school communities constituting the inner section districts of any large urban city. Excluded with equal effectiveness have been the voices of the powerless poor, as well as those of the powerless Black, the powerless students, and other powerless minorities of all descriptions.

The relatively voiceless state of these communities the education enterprise purports to serve is not the only casualty of prevailing political schema. It is only the beginning. Quality, flexibility, climate, and change are all sacrificed, while the politically volatile question of salaries arises, every year, to consume dollars that are becoming increasingly difficult to acquire.

Involved, in addition to the many white elephants carried on the shoulders of the education enterprise, are powerful pressures to build new buildings, rather than explore new physical environments for pursuing the goals of education.

Another complicating factor is a kind of *de facto* segregation in the schools, damaging through separation of children of different economic classes. Because of the failure of education to meet the proliferation of contemporary challenges described in these pages, a pattern now exists which encourages and permits affluent communities to "zone out" families who cannot pay their way in terms of local property taxes.

Thus freedom of choice is denied to many Black families and their children who wish to move out of the central city but cannot because of a variety of exclusionary practices. A related factor with respect to suburban communities is denial of the basic principle of equal educational opportunity, since the tax bases of different communities produce school systems of widely varying quality. The tax system prevailing in most communities compounds all other problems. Communities with large numbers of low-income families are forced to attempt to provide services with inadequate funds resulting from a restricted tax base.

The regressive character of the present system for financial support to the schools also leads white families on stable or declining incomes to be suspicious of any proposal for increased government spending, even to benefit their own children, much less to benefit the Black, brown, red, or yellow.

One major way to overall improvement in education for the Black and the poor is to make the funding of schools dependent on a less regressive and less localized tax. A statewide system of financing should be instituted, with revenues redistributed on a per-student basis to the districts of the state. Special financial provision must be made for educationally depressed areas. There is also a need for state and federal action to prohibit the kinds of local regulations that now perpetuate both exclusive schools and impoverished schools.

An important vehicle for both the change of attitudes and the institution of specific programs is improved organization in the Black community. Active and enlightened school programs are much more likely to result if Black parents themselves are enabled to develop a greater sense of involvement. If greater involvement of the Black community were developed, and if improved processes for local community participation in planning were created, improvement of schools would be more easily attained and school programs would be more effective.

As another variable determining the frustration index for the Black community, if the justice system would straighten itself out the problems of education would be less complex. At the moment the probability is far too great that a school-age Black male youth will spend at least some time in penal custody. The price for indiscriminate assessment of this penalty is prohibitive. For the many, a term in jail is financially penalizing insofar as income is concerned. It may well be the single greatest cause for termination of formal education in the Black community.

The import of a successful student to any community can be documented by available statistics. A student graduating from college can expect to earn, during his lifetime, approximately $475,000. One finishing high school will earn something like $250,000; and those completing grammar school, $150,000. It is clear that a high premium is placed upon education in the present society. Even considering the law of averages, a student who is barred from a college experience can expect to be barred also from earning an extra $225,000 during his working years.

As the gates to further schooling close before him, the gates of opportunity also close in front of the Black youth who has "done time" or simply been discouraged by the circumstances of his life experience.

Fully aware of his powerless state, and impressed by it, he too often has little faith in his ability to confront power figures alone or in a rational way. This is why there has been a tendency toward group action accompanied by abrupt language that is often lusty and frequently insulting to the target of their complaints. The desired shock effect is psychologically supportive in a variety of ways. Above all it tends to engender the same apprehensions and uncertainties within the listener under attack that is part of the daily experiences of the Black youth himself. This phenomenon is apparent even among Black students who survive the system and make it to college.

The oral-oriented confrontation style of the Black youth, in jail or out, in reacting to his depressed condition is related to a basic life-style characteristic that emphasizes the spoken word as a most potent survival tool. Very often it is the only tool he possesses. Administrators should not panic, therefore, when the spokesman for a rebellious group of Black youth launches an invective; larded liberally with "motherfuckers" and "bullshits." Neither should they react with punitive intent. The youth, spurred by regular expressions of "Right-on" from his cohorts, is expressing his manhood, as well as his anger. Underlying this is a veritable plea for understanding, justice, and an educational program that caters to his strengths rather than his weaknesses.

Testifying in behalf of the creation of a national institute for educational research, Daniel P. Moynihan, former presidential assistant, stated that the ambitious educational programs of the 1960s, especially those sponsored by government, "haven't done what was expected of them." He attributed their failure to insufficient knowledge about the "learning process" and to broad, attractive assumptions which simply have not held up. He challenged the belief also that reducing the teacher-pupil ratio and putting more and more money into education would infallibly improve its quality. Moynihan's views are sound in every possible way.

Curriculum effectiveness and the tailoring of instruction on an individual basis for all students (Black, brown, yellow, red or white) are inseparable in any learning environment.

An effective learning environment for Black students, perhaps all students, is among other things a place where people have the background, competence, and freedom to explore comfortably in order to seek answers or solutions to well-motivated questions or problems bearing on their existence. This is in contrast to the traditional school setting, where Black youth are taught to ingest whatever is offered through a teacher. Even the most creative teacher can destroy any prospect of learning by making all educational decisions for the Black student instead of providing the realization that he has decision-making powers and some control over his destiny, and the opportunity to learn from his own mistakes.

A most promising factor in revitalizing the educational process as it affects Blacks, the poor, and other minorities, as has been described earlier, is the community educational institution (the community school and college). Marked by maximum local control and decentralization, flexible grade divisions, heavy emphasis on developing individual potential, individualized learning formats, classrooms without walls, and full integration into the school plan of all community resources, the community educational institution may surely be the instrument of responsiveness needed in contemporary urban settings.

As has been discussed earlier, schools operated through absentee administration, only remotely familiar with the specific characteristics of a particular neighborhood, can never be absorbed into the conceptional frames of reference on which the idea of community schools can be built. Neither is a situation an acceptable component of a community school where teachers "rush-in" on expressways from the suburbs to occupy school buildings for a specified number of hours. The pattern of alien "rush-ins" who "rush-out" with frantic haste at the closing bell provides one of the major reasons for the general hostility existing between school and community.

To repeat, the true community school provides built-in safety features to handle its own failures, staffing patterns that blur the line demarcating professional and nonprofessionals so as to permit full community interaction. This includes the accrediting process, participating as indigenous counseling and instructional personnel, and providing inputs for meaningful curricula that can respond swiftly to new events and ideas. It must also provide for a 24-hour per day, seven-day per week participation in community development.

In most of the areas of this country, particularly the urban and suburban sections, multiple ethnic, social, and religious groups flow in interweaving streams. It is, therefore, imperative that token modification of curriculum be replaced by an actual accommodation of racial and ethnic differences. The new community school can do this. All schools must acquire the same capability.

Token modification of curricula must be replaced by massive infusions of new materials and experiences reflective of the wide variety of human behavior conditions, contributions and values which make up the cultural backgrounds of citizens in a truly pluralistic society. Required also are some changes in attitude about human potential and what the average individual can be expected to accomplish.

At the present time only about a third of the nation's students really master the skills and concepts presented to them in school situations, but 95 percent are capable of doing so. Most of them do not master these skills because they are neither expected to nor given a genuine opportunity to do so. The entire system, in fact, is based on the assumption that they will not succeed.

A major problem we are elucidating is that the concept of public education is slowly changing from identifying promising students to educating everyone without regard for color or economic status; however, the policies and practices have not changed in recognizing this emerging fact. But the greater problem goes deeper still. Education in a pluralistic society must provide exposure to and choice among a wide variety of values, content, and experience with protection of the student's right to examine, criticize, and reject. Information mastery, communicative competence, problem solving, and personal-social self-mastery are also highly relevant as educational goals. It is the manner in which these are usually represented in the curriculum that are irrelevant to the Black student's concerns.

How to change the system and develop human potential on a broader scale to include the "have-nots" has been discussed intensively by Benjamin S. Bloom, professor of education at the University of Chicago. In an article printed by the UCLA Center for the Study of Evaluation of Instructional Programs, Bloom suggests that the major villainy is stubborn adherence to grading practices which automatically insure that only about one-third of a given class will be considered as having achieved anything approaching mastery of the subject.

"If we are effective in our instruction," Bloom writes, "the distribution of achievement should be very different from the normal curve"—that is, most students should get high marks. The present system tends to convince many, Black students in particular, that "they can only do poor or failing work."

The fact is that not all students in a class, Black or otherwise, are interested in the same areas at any one time. Especially in schools attended by minorities, students bring widely differing levels of competence, social awareness, and psychological or academic readiness.

One answer is to stop using individual differences as a means of determining who does well in group competition and start using them as a means of varying teaching techniques to ensure the individual's success in learning. Aptitude differences, for example, traditionally considered a measure of capacity to learn a given subject, now appear to be more accurately a measure of "the amount of time required to attain mastery of a learning task."

What the "problem schools" ought to be grappling with in relation to aptitude are: (1) ways to reduce the time required for mastery by the slower students, and (2) appropriate environmental and learning conditions to improve learning efficiency.

Still another consideration is the growing awareness that education must now prepare students for work that does not yet exist, and whose nature cannot even be imagined. This can only be done by teaching students how to learn, and by giving them the kind of understanding that will enable them to apply accumulated wisdom to new conditions as they arise. In other words, every learning experience must be designed so that the student can learn by exploring, discovering, and deciding. If procedures in schools are changed so that when a student so desires he can involve himself in decision-making and intellectual exploration, he not only will have the opportunity for superior learning, but also will have the freedom to learn when and what he wants to learn.

But, again, different students need different types of instruction—independent study and one-to-one tutoring, for example.

It is also clear that a student cannot learn effectively if he cannot understand the instructions and materials presented to him. Employing a great variety of materials, using teachers who can communicate, and encouraging students to learn cooperatively in groups of two or three are ways of avoiding this difficulty. Learning is the important thing, and instructional alternatives should exist to enable all students to learn the subject at the highest possible level in the knowledge that the citizen of tomorrow will never be in a position to cease learning.

As Bloom has stated: "Mastery learning can give zest to school learning and can develop a lifelong interest in learning. It is this continual learning which should be the major goal of the educational system."

New forms of liberalizing education must also become ideal agents in the effort to end the negative associations attached to the word *Black*. The terms *Afro–American* or *Black* are products of a new power of awareness of internal private dignity. As indicated earlier, Black people in this country are in the process of redefining themselves and their relationships to other human beings in society. Education must contribute to the achievement of these goals and establish the environment necessary for developing the desire to learn.

By recruiting sensitive teachers with the attitudes, information, and skills to bring a balance between the needs for development of the hearts and minds of Black youth, education *can* be made continually relevant to Black people. One most effective avenue is obviously through actual hiring of Black staff.

The recruitment of minority persons by an enlightened school should be based upon a commitment to hire at all levels, not just teachers (that is, clerical, secretarial, administrative, as well as faculty), because students need this kind of broad exposure as aspirant figures for upward mobility. Black persons must be fully integrated into the staffs of new educational prototypes in numbers that at least reflect their percentage in the general population. Not the least important reason for this is that the multicultural visibility this will provide is a most important source of new levels of interracial understanding.

Needed in addition to teachers, administrators, and others are Black "community counselors" to help students cultivate attitudes necessary to lead worthwhile, humane lives, as well as to help them master the skills essential for meeting the problems of survival tomorrow. Black counselors besides empathizing with students can keep open the lines of communication between the Black student community and staff. Obviously, the Black counselor must himself be a well-adjusted individual with whom the minority student can identify in discussing school problems, not a confused member of the Black bourgeoisie who is still trying to come to peace with himself.

The major requisite for producing more Black graduates at the college level is liberalized admission policies that are honest in intent. It is a fact now that a majority of Black students are being denied college entrance because of such irrelevancies (at least for them) as entrance examination scores and high school rank. In truth, this *is* an absurdity of the highest order. Yet efforts by some educators to reform current admissions practices are being stymied by atavistic thinking smacking of racism.

A prominent government official in reacting to a move by the University of Michigan to make admissions practices honest underscored prevailing attitudes among many elitist-oriented racists by asserting that education for leadership should be reserved for the upper and middle classes. Such an attitude is ridiculous.

Education for obsolescence or second-class citizenship, it must be admitted, has always been the lot of the Blacks, the browns, the reds, the yellows, the have-nots of this country. And vocational education, narrowly defined, has usually been the euphemistic title of programs that were dead-end and recommended for them by those holding an elitist view.

Despite the Agnews, Shockleys, and Jensens, however, a new view of Black potential and equal opportunity has begun to emerge, combined with an equally new view of occupational education. This new view blurs the lines of demarcation between vocational-technical education and so-called professional education. Career education is now being thought of in a way that creates new opportunities for those previously excluded through the vocational-technical doorway.

Aiding the emergence of this new view has been the "New Careers" phenomenon, an explosion of paraprofessional opportunities which has made possible a drastic change in the career ladder in such areas as medicine and business. Under the new arrangement the first step in the career ladder could be a short-term technical program of one kind or another meeting the requirements of being open-ended and articulating in a fluid way with programs of greater length.

In the health area, for example, a student could begin by seeking a two-year degree as an inhalation therapist or physician's assistant, proceed into a four-year program to earn a traditional bachelor of science degree or the new one in bachelor of medicine, and proceed further to earn the M.D., all of this in six years.

Similarly, a student could initiate a two-year program in accountancy, computer science, or midmanagement; proceed to completion without massive loss of credit to a four-year degree, and continue to the master's degree or even the PH.D. Admission to a graduate program will soon be possible immediately after

completing two undergraduate years in a college such as Malcolm
X College.

Important to the development of the new education concepts
involved in all of this is a series of new relationships among certain of the community colleges, universities, and professional
schools. In Chicago, for example, Malcolm X College, of the
City Colleges of Chicago, and the University of Illinois–Circle
Campus signed an unprecedented mutual assistance pact. This
agreement permits a student at Malcolm X College to enroll simultaneously at University of Illinois and be considered a full-
time student at both. It is anticipated that a combined degree
from these two institutions of Bachelor of Arts or Science will
be approved eventually by the State Board of Higher Education.
Already institutions outside Illinois are working with Malcolm
X College on this basis. Included are the University of Massachusetts, Antioch College, and Rutgers State University.

Preliminary to the concurrent enrollment agreement, the University of Illinois reviewed all of the courses at Malcolm X and
agreed to accept as transfer credit 99 percent of all credits offered, thus shattering, forever, it is hoped, the elitist notion of
traditional programs as superior to the creative program generating out of institutions committed to the idea of an education of
excellence and relevance for Black people.

The combination of these new developments has raised the
status of the community college from junior partner to equal
partner. The community college in its new role is viewed, in
other words, as having "co-opted" the immense oligarchy that
heretofore has dictated all directions for higher education. It has
assumed the role of leader in making education relevant and possible for the alienated masses of undereducated and underem-
ployed.

This development imposes new obligations on leaders of community colleges. Every community college must now combine
job analysis, job development, and job placement with the traditional obligation of facilitating progress toward advanced degrees. It also inherits a responsibility to recruit the student,

recruit the job, sometimes create the job, and match the two, complete with appropriate credentials, before claiming to have even partially fulfilled a mission with respect to the individual student.

The counselor in this kind of college must be given the status necessary to operate on an equal basis with other school representatives.

The "good teacher" in the community college must be redefined as one who understands white racism and institutional racism, and who is highly sensitive to the needs of the students and the community. Such a "good teacher" must understand that every Black learner says, in effect, "I am ready and eager to learn, but what you have to offer must be personally significant to me, appropriate to my present level of growth, and related to my goals for the future."

A further characteristic of the kind of contemporary educational enterprise now emerging is highly individualized study programs under maximum decompartmentalized conditions. Another is the development of a system that provides the student with a sense of what society expects in the way of performance.

Any educational system that is lax in its demands will lead the student to believe that such are the expectations of his society. If much is expected of him, the chances are that he will expect much of himself. The idea of excellence is becoming an overriding concern of the Black community.

But again, revitalization of our educational system will never achieve full bloom unless the archaic practices that have guaranteed an inferior education for Black people for too many years are relegated to the junkpile where they belong. The challenge for faculties and administrators is very clear. Either an enlightened spirit of determined creativity will spearhead an educational revolution or the educational system will continue to settle into a mire of ineffective mediocrity that is already becoming its chief characteristic.

To overthrow characteristics that have caused public educa-

tion in this country to become the favorite whipping boy of the
left, the right, as well as the middle, will take more than courage.
Educators who would lead American education out of the present morass and into a future of equal opportunity for all people
must have sensitive awareness of past weaknesses, and of the new
populations which must be served. They must also be willing to
set some bold new goals and achieve them, even though the task
will not be easy.

Let's set the record straight on violence. The truth of the thing is that almost without exception all the violence in America comes from white people. White people have made every decision about every war we've been engaged in—the Civil War, the two World Wars and the mess we're engaged in now. White people killed Abraham Lincoln, John Kennedy, Robert Kennedy, Martin Luther King.

Black America has said in a thousand ways that it believes in America. It has said it in slavery, it has said it in war, it has said it in peace. It seems to me the time has come for America to say . . . "Black Americans, we believe in you."

Whitney Young

5

WORKING SOLUTIONS

Following the assassination of Dr. Martin Luther King, Jr., the frustration and rage of a grieved Black community exploded in an expression of despair that shocked all of America, and in fact the entire world. At last the façade of patience with the gradual but slow improvement in the life conditions of Black people had been ripped away. Revealed in its place was a condition of indignation, frustration, despair, and anger—generated by the sordid situation of life in the Black ghetto.

Fires tinged the night skies pink, and cinders mixed with the stars to create the illusion of a fiery inferno in which all of the sins of time, apathy, and unconcern were being consumed in symbolic retaliation against an invisible enemy. The response, in the form of armed troops in battle regalia, accompanied by tanks and other armored weaponry, was swift and repressive.

The fires soon smoldered and the cinders cooled leaving burned out shells of slum dwellings as ragged monuments to the sudden rebellions. But out of the holocaust came a new awareness on the part of all of America, if not the entire world, that the contented Negro of earlier decades had turned into an angry figure of Black rage. Temporarily evicted, the slums and their residents waited restlessly for some positive effects. They did not come.

As matters now stand, the outlook for the underprivileged ghetto youth of the large city and also for the deprived poor of outlying areas continues at very best unpromising. They are still bound within the impersonal operations of a vicious circle. Unless their ability to get and hold decent jobs is improved substantially the fires may again flame the skies signalling the start of a new Armageddon.

The educational inadequacies of ghetto youth have always been intimately related to their inability to compete successfully for jobs, and to enjoy other channels for upward mobility. These youth, aware of the increasing demand for technical competence that results from conversion to automated processes, face the dismally real future of being unable to support themselves independently. Indeed, as the requirements for employment rise, the level of school achievement for the typical ghetto youngster has actually diminished. Moreover, the kinds of jobs that have been traditionally available to those of modest educational achievement are the very sources of unemployment created by the introduction of automated processes. Those jobs that require considerable specialized training, training that most young men from lower income settings do not have, are the present sources of employment.

The employment picture is even more shocking when one realizes that more than 26 million new workers will be added to the American economy during the present decade—this in a period when machines now have the high school diploma.

What does it all mean? It means that one-third of the young people in the United States are coming into the economy bitter and disillusioned because they are unable to function in it decently. Unless something is done, in the present certificate or degree-conscious society, a far more potent explosion of human rage is inevitable. The only alternative is a repressive welfare state characterized by new forms of civilized slavery.

Although advanced training and higher education in the past were prohibitively expensive for the disadvantaged youth, the picture is beginning to change because of the burgeoning increase in publicly supported community colleges across the country. Much encouragement derives also from the rise of a wide variety of "open ended" technical and occupational curricula that can be completed in two college years or less and which articulate efficiently with curricula leading to bachelor degrees.

The true import of the comprehensive community college for undereducated and poverty-stricken ghetto youth can be realized, however, only after delving into the social and economic circumstances described in earlier chapters.

It has in the past been virtually impossible for Black youth to break out of the vicious cycle currently operating. Not only has the outlook been bleak for them, the prognosis for their children is even more foreboding unless massive intervention ensues promptly.

This is the reason why one can anticipate, if not more long hot summers, some other expression of the extreme dissatisfaction with existing conditions by thousands of poor Americans, especially Black Americans. If the prevailing vicious circle is to be broken, it must be done through such exterior forces as specially devised occupational programs offered by the comprehensive community college.

The school has always been an integral part of the insoluble problem of low-income Black youth. On the one hand the school denies them education with any promise for access to success, yet they are urged and warned that they must stay on to graduation if they expect to get any kind of job. They are lectured about democratic processes, but have little or no choice in determining the course of their own lives and in the process are denied dignity and often stigmatized or ostracized.

The response of low-income Black youth to schools which present bitter contradictions resembles the behavior of other organisms presented with insoluble problems. They engage in irrational behaviors, and sometimes flail out wildly, even at their friends.

The problem for too many of these youths is not only that they lack future orientation, but indeed that they feel they lack a future. They are made aware of this early since there is so little meaning in their lives.

Because of its concern with providing professional or technical education in a truly humanistic setting, the community college will probably lead the way to the first truly significant changes in American education since the birth of land-grant colleges. For the student with a purpose there should never have been a conflict between the technical or vocational training he needs and the kind of liberal education that will help him become a better human being.

The philosophy of a "properly constructed educational program" should emphasize the need to guard against educating human beings for technical obsolescence. Although it is vitally important to provide an individual with a marketable skill, it is equally important that he have the potential for greater flexibility and for maximum economic viability.

The curriculum which contains the kinds of studies implied here will foster experiences which are significant in the individual lives of the students and at the same time relevant to the needs of the society in which the student lives. So, in addition to developing the skills of a subprofessional, paraprofessional, or professional, the aim in the occupational curricula must be to develop a person who can think critically and creatively about this society and form proper standards of taste and judgment in connection with the culture which surrounds him.

The heart of the matter is simple: a major responsibility of the comprehensive community college is to train millions of young people for survival and at the same time provide an historical perspective and insights into the elements of logic. There certainly should be few curricula that do not lend themselves to this kind of exposure.

Essentially, one could agree also that the problem in provid-

ing occupational educational programs that produce truly educated people resides in getting the proper kind of teachers—the
kinds of persons who can teach specialized areas in a way that
helps students develop open minds and a respect for views different from their own. Unfortunately most two-year colleges today
provide education that is as invalid as the more traditional curricula in four-year institutions. There must be, at least for the
Black student masses, a profound liberating element designed
especially to help them understand the circumstances surrounding their lives, as well as to learn to do something about improving the lot of their general community. Such programs must
reflect an understanding of the background of the new attitude
emerging in Black communities.

Most significant is the view held by Black people that they
can no longer look to integration as the solution to their problems. They view themselves as being in the process of building a
whole new self-image and a whole new way of life. Thus, they
are in the midst of a Black Cultural Revolution where Black
consciousness is already a reality. Black youth have become
aware that being Black makes them in an almost literal sense
people separate and apart. Even in high school these young people are reveling in their identity. They are forming a sense of
identification with the history and culture of Africa that helps
them realize the Black man's history did not begin on a slave
ship.

Self-determination is the basic thing that Black people are
working for and fighting for everywhere in America. Educational
programs must prepare Blacks to participate in this struggle. Academic courses must be designed to clarify and strengthen, not
destroy, knowledge of Black consciousness and Black pride. As
the youth hungrily seek an understanding of self, their trust must
not be betrayed. Somehow the total learning situation must be
revolutionized to accommodate their mistrust of the system, as
well as their need to meet the demands of requirements for employment in an increasingly technological society.

In the past, the basic failure of schools with Black youth has been their inability to motivate them properly. Educators have made elaborate studies and conducted comprehensive tests to find out why Black youth are not motivated. The answer is simple. Black youth can be motivated. Black youth can learn. But Black youth must understand that they are learning to help the Black community. Black youth know that as individuals they cannot escape from second-class noncitizenship. You cannot motivate a Black youth by telling him to work hard so that he can become the biggest inferior Black man in town. The Black youth says by his every act that if he cannot be a man with dignity and power, he would just as soon be nothing at all; further, he knows that he cannot be free until his entire community enjoys that same privilege. Therefore, his education must prepare him to do both: free himself and his community. Properly constructed educational programs can achieve these aims efficiently and effectively.

At the moment the existing institution that holds greatest promise for fulfilling the potential of the model described here or of becoming the model itself *is* the community college, especially as represented by Malcolm X in Chicago.

Community colleges must be without a doubt the leading edge of any real desire to extend opportunity for higher education to all citizens. This is, of course, an educational *mission* of high import.

Community colleges properly constructed can (1) enable the local community to develop new social ideas and the goals and technology for handling its special local problems; (2) provide courses and formats of education which are suited to the interests and needs of particular clientele; and (3) incorporate a variety of very different kinds of educational enterprises for the present and future.

These colleges generally began as extensions of high schools. In time, they became autonomous units governed by local boards. Now they are assuming "rightful" prestige as institutions of significance and excellence.

The community college is probably the most striking development of the century in higher education. Its impact may be measured by the fact that in 1970, 30 percent of all higher education enrollments (well over two million) were in community colleges.

The Carnegie Commission on Higher Education also notes *that community colleges have exciting possibilities, but caution that their promise is rapidly being undermined. Above all, it is agreed, a community college must avoid becoming a repetition of its predecessors, or so determined to be all things* to all people that it evokes no response at all.

Significantly, the four-year colleges and universities are shifting more and more responsibility onto the community colleges for undertaking the toughest tasks of higher education. Simultaneously, *"the problems of the (1) poor match between the student's style of learning and the usual style of teaching, (2) pressure to attend college directly after high school, (3) continued overemphasis on credentials"* are impairing the ability of community colleges to perform the immense tasks they have been given. It has been pointed out by numerous reports that the two-year institutions are not yet set in concrete. It is imperative that inflexible molds not be formed. *Already, however, many community colleges have been converted in fact and in the public mind from community institutions to "junior colleges,"* a dangerous misnomer.

Malcolm X College, a state and municipally supported community college in Chicago is perhaps one of the most revolutionary departures from the classic mold of education in America, even among community colleges. Growing out of a combination of the times and a bold staff in the college itself, it may be one of the brightest lights of new hope for education at every level.

The college, described by many as a truly humanistic institution, is dedicated to educational excellence for purposes of freedom, equality, and justice for all people. Essential constructs in the philosophy of this predominately Black college include for each individual irrepressible dignity, enduring honor, unquench-

able courage, and undying love for humanity. On these foundations the college strives to build the individual's need to cope
with the future *and* assure the future of his community.

The following excerpt from the college's catalog is illustrative
of the way in which this particular school departs from tradition:

> We are a community of equals, dedicated to the causes of
> equal opportunity and brotherhood. We are committed to serv-
> ice as a way of life and expect all members of our community to
> be actively involved in meaningful service activity. Teachers and
> staff are expected to engage in community service as a condition
> of employment; students are expected to do so as a requirement
> for graduation. Usually, the community services required can be
> combined with classroom or regular employment duties. But
> many in the college, staff and students, will want to go far be-
> yond these levels in the interest of freedom for all people.

Programs offered at Malcolm X College (see appendixes) reflect the dissatisfaction of the Black community with many of
the traditional methods of approaching the problems of educating the disadvantaged. Black educators have learned, for example, that (1) the traditional-type remedial courses to compensate for the years of previous inferior education only create
a demeaning self-image; (2) failing Black students does not motivate them to try harder, but reinforces their failure expectancy;
(3) special compensatory efforts must permeate every separate
component of the entire college program and be carefully co-
ordinated in order to meet the unique needs of Black and low-
income students.

The following are other essential features of an ideal educational paradigm for an oppressed community:

    1. Instruction designed to satisfy the needs of individual
students

    2. Clearly, written course objectives to guide students,
instructors and administrators

    3. Evaluation of a student's performance determined by
his achievement of pre-set objectives

    4. Adjustable time limits for achieving course objectives

5. A continuous admissions program that will bring as many students as possible into the college in a given time period to utilize all available space. Programs available to students at times when they can take advantage of them

6. Continuous evaluation of instructional effectiveness

7. Course credits given on the basis of life experiences for adults entering the college and for learning achieved in non-formal school settings

8. Learning opportunities provided seven days a week.

Black people of America deserve the best that education can produce, not the worst. Essentially, therefore, it is to the thousands of Black youths and other disenchanted adult poor to which a community college in an urban ghetto must address itself.

As stated in its official philosophy, Malcolm X College is a concept of the future whose past is rooted in the enslavement of Black people. "So pervasive is the heritage of slavery in this society," the philosophy asserts, "that we must constantly struggle to keep from unconsciously allowing to develop at this institution situations which serve to enslave and to exploit rather than to develop and actualize human potential."

The processes by which "ideal" slaves are made is described as follows:

... [a setting of] strict discipline. . . .
... a consciousness of personal inferiority. . . .
... a sense of the [system's] master's enormous power. . . .
... an interest in maintaining the status quo and an acceptance of alien standards of good conduct. . . .
... a sense of their helplessness . . . and a habit of perfect dependence upon their masters.

Clearly, to avoid perpetuation of the system's psychological and social enslavement of any people, mechanisms must be developed, articulated, and practiced which will serve to liberate— teachers as well as students.

Such mechanisms as the following must be instituted:

The understanding that discipline follows from a precise understanding of what must be done and why: it generates from within the individual and the group and must be enforced by each individual in the group.

A deliberate effort must be made to develop a capacity to master whatever one aspires to learn and to succeed in whatever one aspires to do.

Those in positions of authority must endeavor to empower their colleagues and subordinates, teaching them how to use power for the good of all.

The enterprise must be viewed as belonging to the people; specifically, to those people in the community who voluntarily express an interest in it—and hence, the standards, norms and values permeate from the base to the apex in terms of the kind of institution desired by the students and the community.

People must be helped to help themselves—to learn from failures rather than seek to avoid them; and must be honored more for having tried than for having succeeded.

Malcolm X College as it exists today is obviously a new kind of institution; one that is in truth attempting to serve as a reclamation center for the human problems created by callously inefficient public schools.

Although it does not discriminate on the basis of color, Malcolm X College is, rather significantly, a Black institution—one in which education services are designed to serve in a unique way the goals of Black people. Programs of the college are designed to promote the Black agenda and "to prepare Black and brown young people to play dynamic and constructive parts in the development of a society in which all members share fairly in the good or bad fortune of the group, and in which progress is measured in terms of human well-being. This kind of college, with a Black-oriented curriculum and philosophy, is in a unique position to deal both with the ills of our society, and the human consequences of its derelictions."

As an integral part of the community itself, the college is creatively and flexibly responsive to the community's needs as well as to those of the individual inhabitants. Where necessary, the college serves as a catalytic agent to synthesize the varied components of the community into a viable force for liberation.

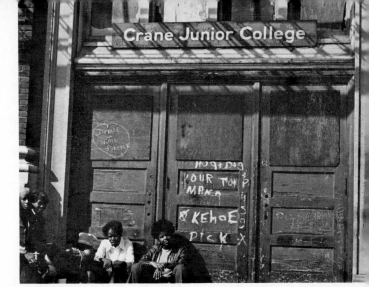

Malcolm X College. Left: as it is today. Above and below: in its beginning [as Crane College].

Photographs by Don Hernandez

Never losing sight of the individual, this institution is concerned at all times with massive changes of social and economic conditions which may enhance the community's potential for successful self-determination.

Creative response to educational needs is the College's most important responsibility. Leadership, where there is a void, and unlimited supportive assistance, where the community has a need, represent the basic tenets of a practical philosophy of commitment that views liberation of any oppressed people as the specific charge for all democratic institutions.

Malcolm X College is attempting to meet the educational crisis in America with innovation, ideas, courage, and a determined will for self-appraisal reinforcing the will for creatively conceived change.

The College rejects the educational process which places didactic instruction at the core, proposing that the time has come to control zeal for imparting knowledge and skills and to concentrate efforts on developing the individual student. A major aim is to promote such qualities as flexibility, creativity, openness to new experiences, responsibility, accountability, and commitment. Similarly, organizational structures are rejected which tend to be paternalistic: "administrators and faculty know best, students know least." The organizational structure of the college is one in which power is shared and the participation of all is guaranteed.

Malcolm X College is called a college of the people—one in which the educational services are designed to serve in a unique way the goals of poor people. Its programs prepare young people to play dynamic and constructive parts in the development of a society in which progress is measured in terms of human well-being, not prestige buildings, cars, or other material things.

This educational model is built upon a different assumption about the nature of potential human ability than is typical of most educational institutions. While recognizing variation, it is assumed that the ability potential of the average Black American is well beyond the normal demand level of the most rigorous academic programs; hence, a maximum social effort is justified to develop the abilities of all people. Concomitantly, any failure to achieve high levels of performance is viewed as a group (social) failure rather than an individual's failure.

The role of staff and students is to remove the obstacles which block the path of those seeking the more specific freedom defined as "the capability to deal creatively and effectively with one's situation."

To assist them in achieving positive freedom, students are encouraged to actively and consciously utilize their personal resources, their life style, and their experiential background in the classroom. The student is taught to become skilled at identifying needs, problems and issues which affect the nature and quality of life in his environment and then use those skills in research aimed at improving the quality of life for him and his people. Essentially, he learns to relate his knowledge to the problems of his community, with a view toward ultimately finding solutions to the community's problems, as well as his own.

Malcolm X College proceeds with its task in the knowledge that racism and discriminations are wrong, irrespective of the identity of the perpetrators or the victims. People should not victimize others or themselves by practices that are legally or morally wrong. All human beings should be invited to share in experiences that create better people and a better society.

After trying in every possible way to meet the vigorous requirements for the type of humanizing educational institution that Malcolm X envisioned, it can now safely be said that Malcolm X College has become an institution dedicated to educational excellence and humanism.

The inherent right of all men to freedom is viewed by all who are a part of this College as so fundamental to the survival of all humanity that the College subscribes fully to the principle of freedom "by any means necessary," as called for by Malcolm X.

Efforts to build a college based upon the humanity of Malcolm X did not always proceed unimpeded largely because many feared that its real objectives might be diametrically opposed to stated ones. Nothing could ever have been further from the truth.

The heritage left to each Black youth by Malcolm included

the responsibility to effect the deeply personal internal revolution that must be the forerunner of attempts to humanize others among them. Not to do this would assure perpetuation of a situation which finds only a few Blacks developing the skills needed to make their communities strong—basically, in the past too many of those few forgot where they came from and never served the leadership function so urgently needed in the Black community. The result has been a Black community without power and frustrated by the futility of such an ignominious condition.

But this condition can change—and has begun to change now with the emergence on to the educational scene of a new kind of Black youth—a Black youth who with dignity, pride, and determination demands freedom, justice, and equality of opportunity —not one who stands hat in hand begging or praying for the basic rights of human existence.

The new Black youth, at Malcolm X and elsewhere, is a restless product of a time unparalleled in the history of mankind. He is a Black youth born in the confusion of the Korean conflict, matured during the futility of Vietnam, and made a man through the fiery revolts in his own streets.

In essence, it is believed that the kind of college represented by Malcolm X, with a Black-oriented curriculum and philosophy, is in a unique position to deal both with the ills of the society-at-large and with the consequences of America's neglect of its minority-group communities.

Socrates once observed, "Our conversation is not about something casual, but about the proper way of life." What we do in education as teachers and students must be judged by society in the light of our quest for a proper and appropriate way of life.

It is society's responsibility to postulate man, not as he has been or even as he is, but as he can be. The task of a nation is to educate men and women to see reality as capable of modification, and above all, to recognize that the efforts of the individual are a part of that reality. They must also be educated in the acquisition and use of power.

And at Malcolm X College is the knowledge that intellectual power is the base upon which all other power must be built.

Malcolm believed rightly that power grows out of a knowledge and appreciation of one's own culture and an understanding of the essentials that historically have been the psychological and spiritual supports of free people.

Malcolm was saying, essentially, let's learn about the pygmies —because pygmies were great freedom fighters. Let's learn about the Massai who were seven feet tall, because they also were great freedom fighters. Let's learn about Denmark Vesey, Nat Turner, and Frederick Douglass, because they too were freedom fighters. And let's talk about freedom as the willingness to pay any price for freedom, the liberation of the human spirit, the liberation of the human mind, the liberation of the Black people, and the liberation of all people.

With this view, he stressed that the Black community must realize that the preparation and preservation of its own youth is indispensable to any community's quest for freedom.

Unfortunately, this country has tended for too many years to respond only to situations of crisis. (The social unrest and agitation of the city riots; the social consequences of rapidly growing crime and delinquency rates; the painful cost of inflated relief and welfare rolls, etc.) Seldom is the enormity of the problems confronting the underprivileged youth in general recognized unless he becomes a part of a crisis. As a result, too many young persons who do not yet belong to delinquency statistics tend to be excluded from the practical circle of rehabilitative programs. Certainly we all ought to recognize that these neglected youngsters who escape police nets outnumber by far those who end up in the jails. Further, they represent the best hope for a profitable investment by a country that can no longer afford to waste its human potential.

In order to right some of the wrongs of the past and avoid unprecedented internal conflicts, rationales for the future must accept the human and practical reality that the masses of underpriviledged youth are not expendable. Black youth, as well as white, from lower socioeconomic settings cannot be abandoned while we struggle for the actualities of a nonsegregated or truly democratic society. During the transition period, something must be done to salvage the bulk of these young people. They must be provided with the skill, sense of personality, stability of character, motivation, and confidence required to achieve and function effectively in a variety of life situations.

In summary, the educational opportunity as provided by the comprehensive community college offers the greatest hope for rehabilitation of blighted ghettos and their inhabitants over the briefest possible period of time. The problem of opening the door of educational opportunity for deprived minority groups is probably one of the most crucial of those facing us in the '70s. Above all, the content of programs at post-high school institutions must be given the quality and prestige that will prevent graduates from being labeled as second-class citizens.

The Black community in particular must avoid such a possibility since it has only recently entered into a new phase of its struggle for liberation from second-class citizenship. In this new phase the Black community is talking about nation-building and educating for self-sufficiency, rather than integration, as was the case during most of the '60s and the preceding decades. The new direction has rather explicit implications for the educational opportunities and the curricula that must be provided. In other words, before a community can become self-sufficient, there is a certain technical and professional competence that must be attained. The training of minority people in most areas has been so seriously neglected over the years that acute shortages prevail in almost any that we can name. The public schools have proved incapable of doing the job to date, and they must reorder their agendas. The comprehensive community college must not imitate that failure.

We will not find a way out of our present troubles until we have the courage to look honestly at evil when evil exists, until we call injustice and dishonor by their right names. . . .

Kwane Nkrumah

6

BLACK HOPE
THROUGH BLACK BOOKS

It may be noted with a sigh of relief that Dick and Jane, the sterling characters of the primary school readers of the first and second grade, have finally been laid to rest. This primary level fairy tale on American life used in our nation's schools for decades will no longer be the official catechism of life in America for millions of defenseless children—Black, red, brown, and yellow. Turning off many completely by its narrow and often hypocritical view of urban life, this book had become synonymous with much of the criticism directed at the schools by Blacks and disillusioned parents of all colors and races from among the poor. Its demise is relevant and significant to change coming about from kindergarten to college.

Even though *Little Black Sambo* and *Uncle Tom's Cabin* have not suffered the same fate, a new day is apparently on the threshold, a necessary evolution if the face of education is to change. The Black revolution in America has begun to hit the publishing industry with a peculiarly reverberating force. As a result of the new demands by school systems for books that portray the participation of Black Americans in the nation's affairs, an unprecedented number of books have been published. Many are remarkably good, historically honest, and intellectually stimulating. Some are superficial and poorly written. This is to be expected.

Many historians of the Black experience and highly critical Black readers will remain unimpressed with most of the new publications, if not incensed. In fact, many in both groups will react with bitter cynicism because of what they consider to be commercialism, attempted exploitation, and shallow treatment of events having deep import to Black people. On the whole, however, it may be agreed the publishing industry deserves encouragement to exit further from its racist postures deeply imbedded in the dark ages of the publishing past.

Although the negative evaluation of the most critical reviewers generally is easily upheld, their criticism is as valid for most literature designed for children and youth as for the present conglomeration of publications concentrating on the Black presence.

As far back as 1939, Kenneth B. Clark and Mamie P. Clark found that Black children evaluated Blacks negatively and evaluated whites positively because of books that excluded Black people or demeaned them. When Lerone Bennett, Jr., wrote a criticism of William Styron's *The Confessions of Nat Turner,* he made this statement about white writers' emasculation of Black families: "First of all, and most important of all, there is a pattern of emasculation, which mirrors America's ancient and manic pattern of de-balling Black men. There is a second pattern, which mirrors the white man's praxis, a pattern of destructuring the Black family. . . ." Bennett's statement applies equally to most other whites who write about Blacks.

Until recently the Black revolution has been too new and too tentative for its values to have filtered down to books for Black children, who are still emotionally and otherwise conditioned by the prevailing white culture through the books used in the nation's schools. Despite the growing number of books depicting the Black experience, the image they give of the Black American is still one of the most insidious influences that hinder the Black child from finding true self-awareness.

The major criterion for acceptability requires that the book communicate to neither a Black nor a white child a racist concept or cliche about Blacks; nor fail to provide some strong characters to serve as role models. The book must also be appropriate for use in (1) an all-Black classroom, (2) an all-white classroom, and (3) an integrated classroom.

The following example is illustrative of the language of racism.

> As you ride up beside the Negroes in the field they stop working long enough to look up, tip their hats and say, "Good morning, Master John." You like the friendly way they speak and smile; they show bright rows of white teeth.
>
> "How's it coming, Sam?" your father asks one of the old Negroes.
>
> "Fine, Marse Tom, jes fine. We got 'most more cotton than we can pick." Then Sam chuckles to himself and goes back to picking as fast as he can.

This description of plantation life in the Old South is found in *Know Alabama*, a fourth grade history textbook now being used in schools across Alabama. The book has come under sharp attack from the National Association for the Advancement of Colored People and a biracial group of mothers in Birmingham. The state superintendent of education says only that he does not consider the book derogatory toward Negroes.

References to the Ku Klux Klan as an organization of "loyal white men" who "knew they had to do something to bring back law and order," apparently will remain in the revised edition, although officials of the publishing firm will not discuss it.

Other sections of the book which have been criticized include an account of Reconstruction entitled "The Terrible Carpetbag Rule." It mentions that Negroes were members of the state legislature, and adds "The Negroes were nearly all field workers. They could not read and write. They did not know what it meant to run a government."

It was very apparent from the content of most of the books

reviewed that the writers were working with one eye on the youth readers, Black and white, and the other on the adult decision-maker, school official or parent. Moreover, the vocabulary and style of most books make it equally apparent that many of their authors relied on secondary research sources for their insights concerning Black linguistic style and the psychological effects of the prevailing Black mood. Some reflected an understandable reticence to cope with the orthographic difficulties of interpolating oral linguistic patterns to printed prose.

Yet there is much encouraging literary potpourri for the Black community and, for that matter, for the white community. In a manner that is sometimes about as subtle as a pounding jack hammer, though not necessarily with that intention, the books spotlight the centuries-old isolation of Black America and the racism inherited as a national characteristic by present generations. At the same time, certain of the new breed of books are refreshingly candid and historically accurate—so much so that they will challenge many teachers who will need to do much homework before assigning these as reading material for their students.

Most refreshing is the new tendency to let the heroes selected by Black people take their place in books alongside those selected for them by white people. Malcolm X, probably the most universally accepted symbol by Black youth of Black resistance to continued third-class status, has now been given precedence over Booker T. Washington and George Washington Carver. This recognition that contemporary Black youth have taken the ideas of Malcolm X as a central guide in their fight for an education relevant to Black people is significant and somewhat inspiring. Equally surprising for some will be the "hero" treatment given to Nat Turner of Virginia and Denmark Vesey of South Carolina, both leaders of slave rebellions.

Running a close second to questions involving the militancy of Malcolm X, Nat Turner, and Denmark Vesey is the treatment of slavery, reconstruction, and post-reconstruction in certain books. Pre-slavery and post-slavery Jim Crowism are now being brought to vivid reality in ways that young Black or white persons can appreciate without becoming blinded by bigotry, bitterness, or hate. One can foresee a time in the future when young Black Americans will come to view with sympathy the morally eroding effects on their persecutors of an extended era where white humans treated Black humans as if they were beasts.

The difficulties of treating these topics on man's inhumanity to man with compassionate justice should be easily recognized. But the relative success of a surprisingly large number of authors has been documented by a variety of Black book reviewers. The consensus of efforts appears in the reviews at the end of this chapter. The books reviewed are only representative of those available by many other equally qualified authors. Further it would not be altogether fair for the remarks to be construed as an effort aimed at literary criticism. Rather they are the reactions of readers who have waited patiently for the "coming of age" of Black-oriented books for use as public school text or as general reading. That time has now seemingly arrived. New Black authors have emerged in a way that is most encouraging for other writers, actual and prospective, in the Black community.

Most importantly, the publishing industry as a whole is apparently maturing in its approach to authors, selection, content, and literary style. It is obvious also that opinions and advice from competent Black consultants are being more carefully followed in a considerable number of instances.

In sum, based on a sampling of recent offerings, the beginning of a new intellectual honesty has become evident in the publishing industry. One result is that future chronicles of Black history and novels based on the experience of Black Americans may be more accurate. This is the kind of foundation upon which interracial harmony can be built.

This time has been a long time coming. Arna Bontemps tells how as a boy about the time of World War I, he went all through the Los Angeles public library looking for some recognizable reflection of himself and his world. What he found was of cold comfort, to say the least, because there was nothing more inspiring on the shelves than *Our Little Ethiopian Cousin*. Even twenty years later, when his children were growing up, Bontemps could find nothing better for them than *The Pickaninny Twins,* so he began writing children's books. The first was *You Can't Pet a Possum* in 1934.

The scarcity of books by Black authors, then as now, was not due to any lack of talent by Black writers. Rather, publishers simply chose to ignore the fact that some 11 percent of their potential customers were Black.

Most American publishers apparently did not begin to under-stand their failures in the areas of fiction, reference books, and textbooks until a few years ago. A number of things happened in 1966 to throw the spotlight on the publishing industry's failures. The Michigan legislature passed a law requiring that the state's schools use only history texts which "include accurate recording of any and all ethnic groups who have made contributions to world, American or the State of Michigan societies." California had enacted a similar law a year earlier.

Congressman Adam Clayton Powell, while still Chairman of the House Education and Labor Committee, held hearings on the treatment of minority groups in text and library books used in the nation's schools. The hearings produced an 800-page rec-ord of testimony. Although no new laws were passed, new pres-sure on the publishers resulted.

A well documented survey was published in the *Saturday Review* during 1966 on racial bias in children's books. The report showed that less than 7 percent of the approximately 5,000 chil-dren's books published in 1962–64 included one or more Blacks in the text or the illustrations. Further, almost 60 percent of the books which did include Blacks were placed either outside the United States or before World War II. In the entire three year period only four-fifths of one percent of the children's books— just eight of 1,000—told a story about contemporary American Blacks. More than a quarter of those showed an illustration but omitted mention of race from the text.

Also in 1966, the late Whitney M. Young, Jr., at the time Executive Director of the National Urban League, attacked both children's fiction and textbooks. He referred in particular to the book, *A Visit to the Zoo,* which shows New York's Central Park zoo in realistic detail except that not one Black face appears in the book, although the zoo is in the heart of New York City and near the edge of Harlem.

All of this helped create a new awareness in the publishing industry. If the need for a change still seems rather evident, it should be noted again that this need only recently became apparent to publishers of children's books.

Executives at a major publishing company surveyed their own books for 1962, 1963, and 1964 and decided that 13 of their all-white books could have included Blacks in a natural way, including the zoo book cited by Young. Another publishing company discovered after a self-study of its works that it had published an illustrated novel about professional football without including a single Black player.

It was in response to complaints about such omissions and distortions that the publishing industry began an active search for Black writers, illustrators, consultants, and editors for its children's books. Progress even now is far below what it should be, but it represents sharp improvement over the past.

In 1970, Dr. LaMar Miller, Director of New York University's Institute of Afro–American Affairs, organized an exhibition of books and reading material for teachers of Black and ethnic studies. He, along with countless others publishing these books, insisted that although there is a rush to the market for Black books, there is some question about their quality.

In other words, there are still few Black editors and there are still questions generating out of problems created when what is published by a Black author has been influenced to a major extent by a white editor. Many Blacks continue to feel that they can't get published if they write about the Black experience and a white editor doesn't understand it. They therefore (at least many) are influenced to write with one eye on the editor and his white opinions.

Generally then, Black writers are agreed that the Black experience is not yet being adequately reflected in children's reading materials.

The president of the American Book Publisher Council was inclined to agree with this view: "Those of us who are white and lead relatively secluded lives, simply cannot judge for ourselves what history and social studies books and perhaps, fiction, are suitable matter. The problem, for us, was not one of intent, but one of a lack of knowledge. We hope we're correcting that."

An obvious need to correct an existing lack of knowledge was what led to organization of the Council on Interracial Books for Children. The idea for the Council originated in 1963. As one of its early contributions, the Council published in its quarterly bulletin an expose of the racial bias in Hugh Lofting's Doctor Doolittle books.

The Council also initiated annual contests to encourage unpublished Black authors to write children's books. Prize winners have all had their books published. One of them, Virginia Cox, won a $500 prize for her picture book. Her book, *The Story of the Alphabet*, put the distasteful past of the children's books and the encouraging present rather succinctly.

The book which had the most profound effect on her early childhood thinking, Miss Cox says, was *Little Black Sambo*.

> During my entire eight years in elementary school, *Little Black Sambo* was the only book about Black people I encountered. Needless to say, I didn't like the book, but it took me years to understand the reasons.
>
> Fortunately for Black children of today, they can read books and look at pictures that more honestly reflect their lives. The main reason that I wrote the alphabet book was to show Black children that the roots of the alphabet used by the Western World originated in Africa. Black children now need to see a positive reflection of themselves in the mirror of history. It is important to show white children that their Black schoolmates have cultural heritage that is important to the development of civilization.

Miss Cox is emphasizing a serious issue when she says it is important to show white children the Black cultural heritage.

The New York Times 45-volume reprint series, *The American Negro: His History and Literature,* also says that "one of the first notions we should reject is that Negro history should be taught only to Negroes. Obviously, American Negro history can provide a more accurate and fully dimensioned picture of our common history in the United States. While Negroes need to know their own heritage, it is a basically academic question whether whites or Negroes need it more."

It is in the areas of history and social science texts that the publishing industry still deserves criticism today. In most standard history textbooks, the Black American simply disappears during the period between the Reconstruction and the 1954 Supreme Court decision. In most of the texts he is considered only as a slave before the Civil War and a problem since that time.

Very few of the history texts trace the economic, social, and political abuses endured by Blacks both in the North and South through the long years before and after emancipation.

History books are not the only type of books, however, which lack appropriate reference to Black people. A well-known professional magazine has noted that "not surprisingly, curriculum areas other than history also fail to adequately deal with Negro contributions to our culture. For the most part, Negro authors, musicians, artists, and scientists are ignored in the English, music, art and science courses."

So while the field of Black and interracial children's fiction is opening up rapidly, the field of textbooks is dragging. Although there is sound improvement, not enough school systems are buying the texts that Black groups consider acceptable—and those which do are principally school systems in large Northern cities.

Several companies are now publishing books designed to supplement existing texts with Black history. But author Dorothy Sterling insists that "history must be completely rewritten, not just revised with supplements tacked onto the end. Seven biographies of George Washington Carver, three of Harriet Tubman, two of Frederick Douglass, one of Benjamin Banneker—it's like a giant jigsaw puzzle with most of the pieces missing."

In an effort to encourage publishers to improve their output, a number of organizations have published lists of approved textbooks and children's fiction. The Council on Interracial Books for Children, in fact, has produced its own listing by analyzing 12 other lists of recommended books for children, but that is not, perhaps, its principal function. One of the most ambitious projects was its involvement with what, until it was abolished, was the Ocean Hill-Brownville experimental school district in Brooklyn. The Council's Chairman took editors from 16 publishing houses to the district as the beginning of a program designed to open up lines of direct communication between children's book editors and the inner city schools. During the tour the editors were told by the supervisor of librarians for the district that: The fact that children, indeed, look for things which are recognizable in their books is reflected in a survey of 30,000 high school students conducted by Baltimore's Enoch Pratt Free Library.

Although the results varied from school to school according to racial composition, the lists of books the students read and enjoyed most since entering high school showed Claude Brown's *Manchild in the Promised Land* second, Harper Lee's *To Sir, With Love* seventh, and John Griffin's *Black Like Me* tenth.

None are considered children's books, of course, but the library commented that the choices "reflect primarily the current interest and concerns of this generation: the adolescent's search for values in contemporary society, love and marriage, the human situation of Black Americans today. . . . indeed, the books being read by the teenager of the present speak clearly of the environment and times in which he lives."

Still, it *is* different now. The several reviews printed below show how and why.

I, Charlotte Fortes, Black and Free, Polly Longsworth, Thomas Y. Crowell Company, 248 pp.

One of the best of the current crop, this book is exciting reading for male and female alike. While containing a social message that is crystal clear, the story of Charlotte Fortes encompasses some of the most breath-taking episodes of the slavery era in the United States. Readers will find themselves so caught up in the storyline that they may not realize the extent to which an astonishing amount of history is being absorbed simultaneously. The tragedy of slavery, the martyrdom of Elijah Lovejoy, the controversy of Harriet Beecher Stowe and her Uncle Tom, the fervor of the abolitionists, the agonizing of Lincoln, the horror of slavery, the stench of war, and the frustrations of hypocrisy, all come to life. Illinois readers may be particularly affected by the Lovejoy section especially because of the present racial bitterness and conflict in Cairo, a small Illinois town bordered on the south by the Mississippi River, where gunfire between Blacks and whites was a daily occurrence in 1970.

Freedom Comes to Mississippi: The Story of Reconstruction, Milton Meltzer, Illustrated. Follett Publishing Company, 192 pp.

That a dream and a nightmare can begin at the same time, or even be one and the same, is vividly portrayed in this concisely written documentary of the period immediately following the Civil War. Despite a tendency to over-simplify complex issues underlying the causes of the Civil War and its aftermath, the author provides a dramatically accurate picture of the first period of "freedom struggle" for Black citizens of Mississippi and elsewhere in the South.

Slave Doctor, Miep Diekman, Translated from Dutch by Madeleine Mueller. William Morrow and Company. 285 pp.

This is the kind of brutally blunt book that plays a role in creating the new kind of youth so visible today. Martin de By, the fictitious hero, would probably be a white campus agitator or a hoodlum priest if he were alive today. This book will not, however, be particularly inspiring for Black youth, although the slaves, Goliath and Nicky, are treated with tenderness and a certain respectful dignity. The book could have been written in the United States, but it is no surprise that it was not.

Young and Black in America, compiled by Rae Pace Alexander. Introductory notes by Julius Luster, Random House.

> The young 13-year-old Black male youth who reads this book will answer his own question of, "Who Am I?" His response will be that I am Frederick Douglass, Richard Wright, Malcolm X, Jimmy Brown, Harry Edwards, and David Parks. His female counterpart will respond similarly by identifying with Daisy Bates and Ann Moody. Crisply written, this well-edited series of profiles is "boss." From the brilliance of Douglass to the incisive candor of reality that characterized Richard Wright the book sparkles. The language level makes this book especially attractive for high school literature classes and selected adult education programs.

Lift Every Voice and Sing, words and music by James Weldon Johnson and J. Rosamond Johnson. Illustrated by Mozelle Thompson. Historical introduction by Mrs. Augusta Baker. Simple piano arrangement with guitar chords by Charity Bailey. Hawthorn Books, Inc.

> A must at every school, elementary, junior high or high with a population of Black students. Its pages are few. But the beauty of the words, enhanced by the inspired drawing art of Mozelle Thompson, makes this treatment of the Black National Anthem one that will be well appreciated by all serious-minded Black people. The creative greatness of the Afro–American was never documented so well.

Nat Turner, Judith Berry Griffin, Illustrated by Leo Carty, Coward-McCann, Inc., 62 pp.

> Nat Turner was the Black Panther of his time. Judith Berry Griffin has written a masterpiece of children's literature in bringing to life the legend of one of the country's most determined freedom fighters. White readers of the book will no doubt develop a new perspective in their views on the Black experience. In this book Nat Turner becomes the hero that Black children need and all people admire. Leo Carty's art work is majestic. The entire presentation is enhanced by the smooth coordination of printed work and dramatic art.

The Black BC'S, Lucille Clifton, Illustrated by Don Miller, E. P. Dutton and Co., Inc., New York.

> A book all young Black parents should own. Reading *The Black*

BC's to the child in the process of learning his *ABC's* will help ensure a strong identification with the history of Black people in America as it really happened. The contributions, great achievements, frustration and suffering are concisely delineated in language that is sometimes beyond the vocabulary of a 5-year old, but nevertheless clear. "H is for heroes" is one good example of daring content which lists Malcolm X and LeRoi Jones. "F is for freedom" shows a Black youth overpowering a white man with a whip. "Z is for zenith" is accompanied by a picture of the black fist—the sign of Black power.

Slavery, from the Rise of Western Civilization to the Renaissance, Milton Meltzer, Cowles Book Company, Inc.

A most scholarly book that never lives up to its potential. The subject of slavery is treated, in this reviewer's judgment, with far too much sympathy and tolerance. The viciousness of the inhumane institution of slavery never really comes through with the force that one would like who continues to experience its remnants in everyday life. As supportive wrongness of traffic in human flesh, it is consistent with historical practice. But for embittered Black readers who are continuing to pay for the questionable morality undergirding so much of western civilization in history, the book simply does not measure up. Despite these strongly-held reservations, the book is probably one of the best treatments of its topic for use in high school, or even for the adult reader who doesn't wish to be burdened with excessive documentation.

Massive studies of slavery as it has existed among mankind must be high on the agenda of priorities set by collegiate institutions aspiring to greatness. Evidence of the extent to which participation in any aspect of human exploitation corrupts and destroys must be made more available by scholars of unquestionable skills. Although this book might be viewed as taking a positive step in the right direction, it would be unwise to view it as more in any event. A skillful teacher can extract a host of provocative exercises from the contents.

I Was a Black Panther, As told to Chuck Moore, Doubleday & Co., Inc.

Earthy. Informative. Perhaps the most moving section is that describing the subject's introduction to Queen Mother Moore (no relation to the author), whose intolerance of the term "Negro" is described in vivid language. The bookstore scene is a

typical genesis in the life of so many Black Americans who
learned for the first time from the new Black bookstore that
there were some books worth their attention. At this point came
the decision of so many to read and to become a scholar on one's
own. The book is real. Its effectiveness is marred, however, by
the deliberate way in which Black language is made palatable
for white readers. This play may help the book avoid puritanical
criticisms for those who continue to live in the world of "Let's
Pretend," but it loses credibility as a result. High school teachers with a modicum of courage should find it earthy and recommend this one as a text or for supplementary reading.

I Wish I Had an Afro, written and photographed by John
Shearer, Cortes Book Co., Inc.

A warmly human peek into Black America, this sensitive accomplishment by talented John Shearer is loaded with forceful
soul. Some pages make one reflect on the accuracy of the old
adage that one picture is worth a thousand words. The pathos
captured by the author's photography is equalled only by the
honest simplicity of the entire work. A Black reader will feel
nostalgic without regret and anger without rage. A white reader
may feel only wonder. For most it will be a peek into a new and
strange world—one they ought to know much better. Every
school library should have this book.

Bitter Victory: A History of Black Soldiers in World War I,
Elorette Henri with Richard Stillman as Military Consultant,
Illustrated by Richard Shore, Zenith Books, Doubleday and Co.

I recall stories told me by my father, one of the first Black soldiers to arrive in France, that were similar to facts in this book.
Most odd to me then, as well as now, is the patient faith in the
future that survives the humiliation of being a Black soldier in a
white army.

To the average American the name Lieutenant Rayford Logan
means little if anything. To a relative few who attended Howard University, Lt. Logan is among the greatest of all Black historians. A scholar, author, and freedom fighter of another era,
Rayford Logan is perhaps the supreme exemplification of the
Black man who went to war in 1917 convinced that by fighting
for freedom in Europe he could induce freedom in America.
Only in his late years did Professor Logan, as I knew him, begin
to entertain some serious doubts about the Black man's "chance

for equal opportunity in his lifetime." The use of Lt. Logan as an example of the trials endured by Black soldiers during World War I gives dimension and added vigor to a book that puts the truth in accurate perspective. Almost brutally blunt, the book even deals with the lies told to Europeans by some white soldiers about monkey tails and other characteristics falsely assigned to the Black soldier.

All the bitterness of Black misery and all the glories of determined participation in the war that was supposed to end wars come to life in this candid dissertation of the Black experience in World War I. Even the fact that the end of the war brought only ridicule and frustration to the returning Black soldier is dealt with straightforwardedly.

Any American reading the book cannot fail to be touched by the poignancy surrounding tales of the 92nd and 93rd divisions. "Ils ne passeront!" "They shall not pass," as words of inspired determination will take on new meaning to Black youth exposed to this part of their history for the first time.

Black Voices From Prison, Doubleday

As the title suggests, *Black Voices From Prison* is a book of prison writings. This is not a book about Black crime or criminality, but is a wealth of selections by and about Black men imprisoned by and often for the profit of whites. It is a strikingly vivid and rigorously clear indictment of the crimes of white society against Black people.

These accounts by poet Etheridge Knight come from a section called "From a Prison Notebook." They, like most of the material by the other writers in this collection, have much of significance in common with early slave narratives of atrocities and outrages suffered, outwitted or defied by our forebears. Narratives of escape and resistance.

The Black Panthers Speak, Edited by Phillip S. Foner, J. B. Lippincott Co.

Dr. Foner, professor of history at Lincoln University, has compiled some of the most forceful writings from the Black Panther journal into a single volume. The writings of Seale, Cleaver, Newton, and Hilliard discuss the Black Panther Party's 10-point program, the power structure and police, and their breakfast program and liberation schools. The volume is also illustrated with Black Panther cartoons.

The Sport of the Gods, Paul Laurence Dunbar, introduction by Charles Nilon, Collier Books, African/American Library

> The reissue of one of the first major protest novels by a Black American, first published in 1902. Dunbar portrays the disintegration of a respectable southern Black family forced to move North. Living in Harlem, the Hamiltons confront violence, brutality, and raw survival only to learn that innocence has no place among the oppressed and vulnerability means death.

The Looming Shadow, Legson Kayira, introduction by Harold Collins, Collier Books, African/American Library

> An authentic African novel which powerfully evokes the love, hate, passion, revenge and retribution of a tribal culture encountering its last and greatest threat—European civilization. A story of witchcraft, the Black Africans who practice it, and their brutal suppression by a white government.

Black Feeling, Black Talk, Black Judgment, Nikki Giovanni, William Morrow & Co.

> The "Princess of Black Poetry" brings together, in one volume, 53 of her poems previously published privately in pamphlet form. Miss Giovanni has been termed the "foremost propagandist" among the "poetry guerrilla fighters" by *Time* magazine. Her poems condemn white racism and exhort its victims to rise up to preserve themselves.
>
> > If the Black Revolution passes you by it's for damned/ sure/the white reaction to it won't.
>
> But at the same time she prefers to be known for the deep affection for Black people that is at the heart of all her work.
>
> > I'm into my Black Thing/And it's filling all/My empty spots.

Backfire: Ordeal at Cornell, Steve Wallenstein and George Fisher, Chelsea House Publishers

> Two student eyewitnesses tell the day-by-day story of the explosion in April 1969 when 200 Black Cornell students seized an administration building and defended it with firearms. Illustrated.

Nipper, Morrie Turner, Westminister Press.

> One of Morrie Turner's "Wee Pals" characters, Nipper presents a satire on adult hang-ups and prejudices built around a baseball team of color-blind little people who may make some readers see through many silly traditions.

Black Means, Barney Grossman with Gladys Groom and the pupils of P.S. 150, illustrated by Charles Bible, Hill & Wang.

> This book is designed to give new meaning and depth and to counteract the negative connotations that have grown up around the word "black." Some of the images created by these elementary school children are: Black is as smooth as velvet; Black is as soulful as the blues; Black is as tender as a newborn baby.

Jim Brown: The Golden Year 1964, Stan Isaacs, Prentice-Hall, Inc.

> 1964 was the year that football's greatest running back led his team, the Cleveland Brown's, to the NFL championship. Illustrated.

Black Preaching, Henry H. Mitchell, Edited by Dr. C. Eric Lincoln, J. B. Lippincott Co.

> Henry H. Mitchell, professor at the Colgate–Rochester Divinity School and a foremost practitioner of the preacher's arts, places in writing the style and approach which have, in the past, been passed from one generation to the next by contagion and exposure. He covers the essential characteristics, cultural context, reliance on the Bible, and the unique language, style and theology of Black preaching. The author also examines the historic and probable future role of the Black preacher as the "natural leader" of the Black community.

A Rap on Race, Margaret Mead and James Baldwin, J. B. Lippincott Co.*

> A Rap on Race is perhaps the perfect example of what can happen when two sensitive and intelligent human beings representing widely divergent worlds engage in a dialogue on a controversial social issue of major dimensions. The acuteness of America's insoluble dilemma, racial conflict, is circumscribed in a remarkably accurate way through the often provocative discussion between Margaret Mead and James Baldwin.

*A rather special review serves the dual purpose of demonstrating the new sense of social responsibility permeating the publishing industry and some of the continuing complexities of reconciling white and Black positions on almost any issue. No more profound plea, unspoken as it may be, could be presented for a revitalized educational curriculum featuring Black, African, and related ethnic studies. The review published here was written by the author for publication in the *Chicago Daily News*, May 29, 1971.

Although the dialogue centers on race, it travels the gamut of human concerns: the Black Panthers, theology, nationalism, war, the Chicago Seven, morality, ethics, women's liberation, human survival, social responsibility, genocide, concentration camps, and even semantics.

The entire book is not so much a discussion between a white and a black as it is a demonstration of how sophistication in one area of human conduct is not necessarily transferable to any other. This is particularly evident in the case of Miss Mead whose credentials as an anthropologist are impeccable. But her naïvete about the problems of blackness, black attitudes, and the nature of black-white issues in the United States become painfully prominent as her responses to Baldwin assume, at times, pontifical overtones.

Disclaimers by Miss Mead of any guilt or feelings of guilt for the many national decisions having questionable moral basis, simply because she had no direct role in making them, are more typical of Nixon's silent majority than of a sensitive social scientist. Consistent with this position, she holds slavers blameless for their part in creating the inhuman practice of selling human beings like beasts.

For many readers of this book, if indeed there will be many, Miss Mead will emerge as the perfect picture of the benign racist. Her statements parallel in so many ways those of other well-intentioned "missionaries." But her attempts to rationalize away this country's inability to cope with its social wounds would get her into difficulty even with the missionary society.

Her universal sensitivity to broad human concern is evidenced many times, however. A strikenly incisive comment on the nature of suffering is quite illuminating.

Baldwin's tenacious persistence in maintaining focus on the survival problems of Black America creates an intellectual continuity in the discussion that makes the book meaningful. Despite his current peripatetic status he continues to exhibit a profound grasp of contemporary positions in the Black community.

Descriptions of the tragedy represented by his early life and the sameness observable today seem to be lost on his discussion partner, who thinks constantly in terms of the good "North" and the wicked "South." Baldwin gently chastises her by citing his agreement with Malcolm X that south in the United States is anywhere below the Canadian border.

The book does accomplish some interesting ends.

First, the curious pathos of the Black American in his relationship to whites and to all other blacks is revealed with a refreshing candor. It is almost as if, in talking to Margaret Mead, James Baldwin is trying to interpolate for all of white America what he really meant in his own writings on the torment of blackness. In so doing, he reveals also the basic flaws in the mantle of morality that has been this country's last line of defense in its justifications for tolerating if not promoting violence as a solution for the ills of mankind. We haven't had five years without violence in America since the arrival of Columbus.

Secondly, a rare consensus found the discussants concluding that the Black man in America is, despite the indisputable African heritage made prominent by the new concern with black identity, an American. In light of this legal fact, continued discussion of the rate at which the full rights of citizenship shall be accorded black people are revealed as another form of the kind of hypocrisy that has alienated the bulk of America's black people.

As a third outcome, and a little surprising at that, the dignity of blacks in America is enhanced. This results in part through Baldwin's description of his early years in Harlem as more typical than exceptional, and in part through Miss Mead's seeming recognition of a unique humanity in black people that has been inherent throughout their presence in America and long before.

Astonishingly, Miss Mead feels that "The (atomic) bomb has given us our first chance at world peace." The contradictions introduced by this statement almost destroy the credibility of all else in the book. On the other hand the courageous anthropologist is probably equally aware that since the "bomb" did not prevent Korea and Vietnam, it won't have much effect in the future as nations continue to find new ways of killing each others' youth.

White readers who label themselves as liberals will probably feel exhilarated as they identify with Miss Mead's positions. Blacks however, will consider them ethically questionable.

Legitimizing as she does certain attitudes that permit evasion of social responsibility, she creates new holes—loopholes.

Yet there *is* an undeniable warmth about this woman. The book brings out a humanity that is either inherent in her as a person or in the experiences that earned her fame.

Through it all, Baldwin exudes the contained power that has marked some of his more outstanding literary efforts. Where one might feel tempted early in the reading of this book to discount his current validity as a spokesman for the contemporary state of black-white relations in America, one is forced into deep admiration for the particularly articulate way he attempts to create new dimensions of understanding for his white conversant.

Despite the feeling that he also suspects that, if she is listening, she isn't really hearing the thoughts behind the words, he is consistently patient, courteous, and respectful. Under the circumstances he could have been forgiven for being somewhat less.

In the end, Baldwin dominates the discussion. The flow of his words generates veritable heat from the pages as his wrath continues seeking a basis for renegotiating the relationships between whites and blacks in the United States. His closing words are thoughts that envelop universal and charismatic appeals.

This is what happens when two beautiful human beings come together, even when one is white and somewhat naïve, and the other is black and toughened by years of thrashing in the mires of black urban bitterness.

The book is worthwhile reading, especially for whites seriously concerned about the inability of the races to reconcile their differences in a peaceful way and engage as countrymen in the pursuit of justice throughout the world for all men.

[The bibliography at the end of this book will introduce interested readers into other areas relevant to the theme of *Passport to Freedom.*]

In summary, Black has without a doubt become beautiful for contemporary Black youth involved in a new appreciation of Black ethnicity. But the Black revolution is still too new and too tentative to take it for granted that its values will automatically filter down to Black children, who are still emotionally and otherwise conditioned by the prevailing white culture. This is why selection of the right books in school and at home becomes so important at every educational level.

*Only when we are clear about the kind of so-
ciety we are trying to build can we design our
educational system to serve our goals . . . [W]e
want to build a . . . society based on three
principles: equality and respect for human dignity; sharing of the resources which are produced by our efforts; work for everyone and
exploitation by none. . . . Only free people conscious of their worth and their equality can
build a free society.*

Julius K. Nyerere

7

BLACK STUDIES

The introduction of Black Studies as a legitimate part of the curriculum is one of the most refreshing educational developments of the 20th century. When this new curriculum is viewed in this light the antagonism of traditionally oriented faculty can be dealt with efficiently. This still new aspect of the response by schools in America to the Black revolution is, despite the loud anguishings of western classicists, based on sound intellectual underpinnings. The major requirements for full success are institutional integrity, the needed teaching materials, and truly competent faculty.

Lerone Bennett speaks dramatically to the need for schools and programs that are relevant to Black people and their experience. He says, "In white-oriented schools, we are educated away from ourselves, away from our people, away from our rhythm, away from our genius, and away from our soul. . . ."

The myth of white supremacy has for long prevented America from acknowledging its African heritage, but the time has come for American schoolchildren, both white and Black, to study the African as well as the European contribution to the language and culture of their nation. There are important differences in these contributions.

While the Western world has cultivated the written word, Africa has cultivated the spoken word, so that by African standards white men frequently appear inarticulate. This important role of the spoken word is preserved among Black Americans. Here we meet one of the ironies of the American situation in which Black schoolchildren, skillful speakers in their own environment, are often assessed as linguistically "backward" by white schoolteachers. Most middle-class Americans, Black and white, regard Black speech as a deviant form of white American English, not realizing that the English used by so many low-income Black people (and an increasing number of those in middle and upper-income brackets) has a longer history than the so-called "standard" American English itself. A "Black" form of English, strongly influenced by Mandingo, Swahili, and other African languages, became established as a trade language on the West African coast from the sixteenth century. Later a pidgin "English" developed in the West Indies and the east coast of the American colonies. Blacks and whites need to know all of this, and more.

Unfortunately, the "slave mentality" of early Black and white critics alike could not at first conceive of a substantive curriculum of studies prefaced by the word "Black," just as they could not see the language style of Black Americans as legitimate. No greater evidence ever was presented of how racism has become institutionalized in the educational systems of this country.

It is most imperative now, in the face of the current crisis in education, that all schools and colleges come to insightful conclusions about the role and content of Black Studies programs. Schools and colleges with sizable Black enrollments in particular, however, need to understand this phenomenon because of its tremendous potential for motivating Black youth, as well as helping to humanize all youth, Black and white.

As James Turner at Cornell has pointed out, Black studies programs can help to decolonize young Black minds and to reorient their minds in ways which allow them to effect lasting, positive, creative relationships between themselves and their community.

The narrowed perspective acquired by those limited to an education based on the "western civilization" point of view has long been one of this nation's Achilles' heels. Further, the deliberate way in which American education and the textbooks it uses ignored for so long Black people and their contributions to American and world culture has helped perpetuate myths concerning racial inferiority.

Students of all ethnic and racial backgrounds need to look closely at the various parts of Africa, from where over 10 percent of all Americans trace their ancestry. They need to know the history of the people who speak Swahili, the tragedy of the Zulus, and especially the history and culture of the great medieval empire of Mali. The language of this empire, Mandingo, is still spoken through much of West Africa and was spoken, either as a first or second language, by a substantial number of African immigrants to the United States. Not surprisingly, the influence of Mandingo can be clearly traced in the development of the American language. A knowledge of Swahili, a language of East Africa, is becoming accepted as an important tool for cultural research in Africa by Africans with American citizenship.

An appropriate rationale for the study of cultural roots has been delineated in these terms: All people should be given the opportunity to know of their unfolding odyssey. And the fact that, at this stage, a demand must be made to include it among the corpus of knowledge to be passed on represents a tragedy for us and a degradation for those who have made this demand necessary. Just as the white American experience would be incomplete and incomprehensible if the history of Europe were to be isolated from it, so also, the total American experience is incomprehensible without the history of Africa. And if the history of the Afro–American is distorted and hidden, then the whole world is short-changed, and the record of humanity diminished.

American people of African ancestry must begin to understand and interpret their historical and cultural experiences as one means of preparing for the future. Black education must also make Black students and their white counterparts consistently conscious of the need for struggle and commitment in connection with the ideals of humanism and full freedom for all people. Too often the question of cultural values and a morally based political ideology are only superficially perceived in this country. James Turner, the eloquent young spokesman for Black studies at Cornell University, emphasized the need to have Black studies as an integral part of all humanities at every level so that sophisticated insights can be developed as soon as possible.

Humanities courses, as they have been taught traditionally, however, have been restricted to western or "white" humanities. This practice has severely handicapped the products of prevailing educational schemes. Similarly, the social sciences have been taught as white sociology, white economics, white political science, etc. Even the natural sciences and mathematics have been contaminated by a racist view which ignores the contributions of non-Western thinking to the storehouse of human knowledge.

African culture and languages are of such great relevance to America that the aim of progressive educational programs all over the United States should be to place the study of African languages and cultures and Africans in America alongside the traditional study of Western European languages and cultures. Such programs would not only provide a more balanced view of the American heritage, but would also give young Americans a better understanding of human societies beyond the confines of the Western world.

Despite high potential, the invigorating experience of a true Black Studies program has not been realized on any meaningful scale except at a very few schools. Interestingly, a peculiar acquiescence by many educational institutions met the early demands by students for Black Studies programs. The students were told to find directors and teachers so the institution could hire them. They were told to structure programs, devise curriculums, and outline courses. When they could do none of these with efficient dispatch, the programs were labeled failures and students were called frivolous. Another case of the self-fulfilling prophecy rearing its ugly head had become a part of our educational history.

Equally tragic were the numerous instances where an institution, announcing new relevance, introduced a course in Afro–American art, changed the title of one called Negro history to Black History, dusted off one called Race Relations, and then laid claims to having a Black Studies program.

As a result, Nathan Hare, former director of Black Studies at San Francisco State, and currently editor of the journal, *Black Scholar*, has said: "We now come to the most crucial stage in the struggle for Black Studies. Though hundreds of programs are bubbling up all over the country, they are falling nonetheless in disarray. They are being corrupted and co-opted in the effort to destroy them."

Dr. Hare's explanation for the present plight of most Black Studies programs should be enlightening for the teacher or administrator seriously interested in an improved overall curricula. But first some background.

Black Studies programs represent the first major change initiated by the presence of Black students on predominately white college campuses. Students have only recently been vigorously recruited by most "predominately white" colleges and universities in the country. Their numbers are still only a token, representing usually three or four percent of the total at best. This highly diluted presence of such a few on the vast complex making up the campus of a college or university guaranteed for a period the high failure-rate that critics of open admissions pounced on so gleefully.

It was psychologically depressing for Black students to find themselves in a setting hostile to them, unprepared for them, and sanctimonious in its toleration of them. Seeing themselves, with much bitterness, as token integrators of racist institutions, even if unconsciously so, they united into Black Student Unions that eventually forced major concessions by college administrations. The Scranton Report described this new unity among Black students as ". . . a developing spiritual and ethnic identity that gives Black students a sense of unity and oneness among themselves and with other Blacks." Out of this background the idea of renewed curriculum relevance was conceived. Its early days were turbulent—in a sense necessarily so.

The new-found togetherness of the Black students generated a militancy in speech and attitude to which the white community was not accustomed and for which it was not prepared. Many initial responses by white educators and others alarmed over this new state of affairs were therefore ill-calculated and militated against the success of early Black Studies programs on school, college, and university campuses. Similarly, the problem of defining Black Studies, its thrust, and the qualifications of the teachers was approached unsystematically.

Just as Dr. Hare has pointed out, most students and administrators did not really understand what "Black Studies" was all about. They mistakenly considered it as synonymous with curricula found at some "predominately Negro" schools where such courses as Negro history or Negro literature appeared regularly.

But Black Studies was never meant to be restricted to the study of the important cultural foundations of a people, their history, their contributions to mankind. They were intended to be, again as Dr. Hare, an early exponent, states, ". . . a pedagogical innovation . . . a new approach to scholarship and teaching which would prepare Black students to function in the hard times ahead . . . while clearing the way for the ultimate humanization of a decadent American society."

With respect to content, Dr. Hare states:

> A Black Studies curriculum must include race analysis, class analysis, and the study of the oppressor as well as his Black victims. There must be study of the march toward freedom of other peoples in other eras and in other lands—why they succeeded, their failures, an analysis of their goals and strategy, their tactics. Beyond this . . . it is folly to omit technical skills (mathematics, engineering, medicine) taught from a Black perspective in, of, and by the Black community.

The statement of definition by Dr. Hare does not deny the valid inclusion in Black Studies programs of courses that enable Black people to rediscover identity, increase self-respect, and in general become aware of Black contributions to humanity's evolution and survival. Neither does it imply that these programs should ignore ancient or modern Africa. The opposite is really the case. Africa has always played an important role in world affairs. It will play a role even more important in years to come. To continue ignoring this great continent would represent national folly of the highest order.

But a Black Studies program must be an invigorating curriculum force, directing academic reform. It cannot consist of "old" courses in race relations, Negro history, Negro literature, Negro music, art, or what have you, and taught by white professors, or Black ones, without appropriate competence.

It would be grievous also if the important relationships of Black Studies courses and programs to the broader community were overlooked. Individuals *must* become sensitive to aspects of their own behavior and attitudes which may obstruct the movement of other people toward freedom. These studies must proceed toward the end that facilitative behaviors and attitudes are developed while those which are obstructive are eliminated.

Prospective benefits are not limited to the Black community. Black Studies courses can, without a doubt, fulfill a need for scholarly correction of social, cultural, and historical myths; provide teachers planning to teach in the Black community with the insights, information, and sensitivity required for success; and prepare future leaders of America for leadership in a pluralistic society. All of this is in addition to the benefits accruing to the Black community in a more immediate way. In other words, the implication here is that Black Studies programs will benefit not only the Black community itself, but the white community as well.

At this point one would have to conclude happily that Black studies are really here to stay. Despite some internal conflicts, Black Studies programs are strongly supported by an increasing number of advocates. As described by Margaret Walker Alexander, Black Studies director at Jackson State College, they are important "By the very nature of their educational and cultural significance. . . ."

At one time the opposing arguments among advocates of Black Studies programs were easily identified by their radical differences. There were those few who espoused a strict diet of so-called "soul" courses, Swahili, and "way-out" philosophy courses. Another group stressed courses in survival and theories of revolution. Still another group favored an Afro–American studies approach including courses in history, music, and arts from the Black point of view. Assailing all these positions were the usual doubters about everything Black people might undertake who labeled all of it trash. Most differences have now been defined as never really having any basis in fact. Controversy was seen as more the creation of detractors than any thing else. The initial controversy was unavoidable, even understandable.

With such a swirl of controversy how could any program survive? Surprisingly to some, a program format *has* evolved out of dogged determination of a cadre of exponents so diverse in its composition as to make it unlikely that one might find them in the same room at the same time. Institutional examples are Harvard University, Ohio State University, Federal City College, University of Massachusetts, Antioch College, Merritt College, and, of course, Malcolm X College.

There is an encouraging refinement of thought on the subject contributed by a diverse group of scholars. In contrast to the fiery revolutionary Nathan Hare, there is Professor Alexander, who while professing no special understanding of some of the more revolutionary type courses states: "I believe there should certainly be such innovative courses dealing with the politics and economics of the Black ghetto; such courses in religion and philosophy dealing with the Islamic or Moslem world; such courses in psychology dealing with the psychotic nature of racism, its basic sickness, diagnosis, and prescription for cure. . . . all students, Black and white, need to know the cultural contributions Black people have made to the modern world in literature, music, art, and religion."

A report by a Yale University group argues: "The experience of Afro–Americans and the relevant historical and comparative experiences of Black people elsewhere furnish an important and relevant body of experience to be investigated by scholars and understood by interested students. This body of experience is of such great variety that no existing arrangement for undergraduate concentration, whether in a department, an area studies program, or a divisional major, can adequately comprehend it."

Even more supportive statements of direction, if sometimes more general, were provided by Orlando Taylor, formerly at the University of Indiana and currently with Federal City College; DeVere Pentony, San Francisco State; Vincent Harding, Institute of the Black World; John Hatch, Cornell University; and Harold Cruse, the distinguished Black intellectual and writer.

Taylor's views of Black Studies grows out of his feeling that: "The present orientation of the American education system has resulted in poor education for Black students, psychological rejection, loss of cultural identity, no feelings of relevance, and denial of cultural needs and aspirations."

He goes on to say, ". . . an Afro–American orientation must permeate the entire (white collegiate) institution. It cannot be a piecemeal program which operates on a shoestring budget. Instead, it must receive top institutional priority . . . should be more than a few courses in Black history and art . . . more than a specialized curriculum." In short, Taylor points out, "The program must be one of total service to the community it purports to serve. It must speak adequately also to all the special problems of those who get into the university: what happens to them and the community while they are there, and what happens to them after they leave. This view encompasses the areas of recruiting, admissions, counseling, financial assistance, academic policies, and curriculum."

Harding, delineating what Black students want, asserts: "They demand experimentation in Black control. . . . They search for answers to problems of funding for an institution unswervingly dedicated to the service of the Black community. . . . They call for new experiments with curriculum . . . saturated in Blackness. They look for ways in which . . . an institution could specialize in research and experimentation toward the rehabilitation of the tens of thousands of Black students who are intellectually crippled each semester in the public schools of the South and the North."

The growing scheme of scholarly thought on the relationship of Black Studies to an education relevant to a community's needs is added to by Pentony, when he says: "The demand for Black Studies is a call for Black leadership. . . . They [Black students] . . . view the college or university as a place where talents can be gathered and resources mobilized to provide intellectual leadership . . . a place for the writing of books, the providing of information, and the training of students to help with the critical tasks. It is . . . one of the testing grounds for the idea that Black people need to have control over their own destiny."

Hatch expresses a similar feeling about the purpose of Black Studies programs: "They must be designed to enable Black people to use the knowledge gained in the classroom and the community to formulate new ideologies and philosophies which will contribute to the development of the Black nation." Essentially the same philosophy emerges from the cry of Imamu Amiri Baraka (formerly LeRoi Jones) that it is Nation–Time for all Black people displaced from Africa.

Inez Smith Reid of Brooklyn College partly assuages the fears of apprehensive whites in saying: "The central push for Black Studies stems from demanding, angry, concerned and constantly troubled young students. Yet, their impatience, their intolerance of slow reactions from administrators, must not allow a program to materialize only as Black matter for Blacks; for it is crucial that such a program become a rallying point where men of different colors and cultures gather to study . . . with an ultimate goal of emerging with a sense of the humanism of Man. . . ."

Whitney Young in a speech before the Congress of African Peoples in Atlanta, August 1970, showed that, encouched in different words, his philosophy of survival does not differ drastically from the functional philosophy observable in the postures on education and Black Studies assumed by Ron Karenga:

> Brain Power . . . is the resource upon which the success of any strategy depends. It is even more crucial for a minority. What

we lack in quantity we must make up for in quality. Brain power to liberate African peoples of the world must be carefully and unemotionally selective.

. . . [We] must reject that aspect of white education which is clearly irrelevant, immoral, lacking in human values, committed to the preservation of the status quo and filled with convenient distortions and omissions of the truths of world history.

. . . [We] must seek the development of an educational content which includes the Black experience, elevates pride and dignity, and engenders a respect for us as a people—past, present, and future. We must reject a self-serving materialistically oriented education which has created and perpetuated the type of leadership which relies on military might as its major appeal for world allies and identifies as its successful and most honored citizens those who possess things, however, immorally acquired.

But the effective brain power also knows what not to reject: Some of the cultural and the esthetic which makes us intelligent artisans; some of the art, the literature, the poetry, the drama that makes us cosmopolitan, aware and sensitive to all cultures; some of the behavioral sciences that make us not only personally aware, but also equally knowledgeable about the weaknesses of our oppressors, as well as the strengths of our forefathers; more than adequate knowledge of the helping professions (law, medicine, etc.) which have little color-component so that we can serve on more equal terms our people who are so severely disadvantaged in these areas.

And, finally, [we must gain] superior knowledge of the economic and political systems that for so long have entrapped and enslaved our people.

Brain power, to the extent I have outlined it, will not be easy to acquire; to amass it in the degree needed will take time. But it is such an essential element in this whole struggle that for ourselves—and certainly for our children—it must become a primary obsession, an all-consuming effort . . . starting yesterday.

So the basis for Black Studies and its validity rests on a sound foundation. Moreover, the confusion cited by many seems to have crystallized into a meaningful frame of reference that will provide the leadership needed by a variety of institutions of serious intent.

But there is one final question. Who shall teach the courses?

The curious dilemma involving who shall teach Black Studies courses occurs at a time when serious questioning is underway concerning the entire process of credentials for teachers. The people "unqualified" to teach in the public schools include such illustrious figures as Ralph Abernathy, Julian Bond, Stokely Carmichael, James Farmer, John Hope Franklin, John Gardner, Charles Hamilton, Vincent Harding, Andrew Hatcher, Jesse Jackson, Lyndon Johnson, Clark Kerr, Richard Nixon, Charles Silberman, Carl Stokes, and Earl Warren. These are only a few of the tremendous number of highly esteemed people who are not qualified by present public school standards to teach in the areas of their specialty. Credentialing practices for many other areas, even for schools and colleges themselves, are equally ridiculous.

Certainly it must be considered ironic that a youth just out of college with 24-credit hours in political science and 18 or fewer hours of "how to do it" courses, but no hours of experience or exposure, is considered qualified to teach the machinations of American politics, whereas a former president of the United States with more years of experience in American government than the recent graduate has years of life is excluded from the public school classroom because he is "unqualified." Even most of our greatest scientists are not "qualified" by the present peculiar criteria to teach introductory science at the elementary school level because of the inexplicable criteria utilized by most public school systems.

Colleges and universities are no less guilty of the same inane behavior. Master's degrees and doctorates are the automatic certificates of entree at this level. It is no surprise, therefore, that perplexities ensue when a new field like Black Studies emerges where no degrees have yet been awarded.

Black Studies courses and programs also caught the complacent American university system flat-footed in terms of teachers. Two alternatives prevailed for the tradition-bound pedagogists in charge of collegiate curricula. Either they could broaden the definition of an existing discipline represented by people already in their faculties to encompass the new offerings being requested or they could raid "predominately Negro" schools for "specialists" who qualified on the basis of race, color, and in some in-

stances titles of courses taught at one time or another. Most
chose the latter course. Needless to say, this brain drain from
predominately Black schools must stop. The contribution of
these schools is too vital. Furthermore, Black faces alone is not
the answer.

Admittedly, the single factor of color sometimes sufficed to
placate the strident voices of recalcitrant Black students demanding relevant teachers and Black Studies programs. But very frequently Black students rejected with contempt Black professors
with white minds and classified solely as members of the Black
bourgeoise; just as unequivocally they rejected the non-Black
professor on grounds of being white.

Only a few universities such as Harvard adopted a reasonable
view as evidenced by the following excerpt from the recommendation of a faculty committee:

> The university should note that many men and women with
> considerable competence and national reputations in aspects of
> Afro-American studies, have not, for various reasons, acquired
> the normal academic credentials. Special efforts should be made
> to invite such people to serve as visiting members of the faculty.

This qualified endorsement of a third alternative for solving
the problem of qualified teachers in Black Studies cracked the
door for less "prestigious" institutions to seize the initiative and
structure new standards. But most were too caught up in the system to take advantage of a rare opportunity to provide creative
educational leadership in truly uncharted waters. Even the community colleges stuttered with indecisiveness when confronted
with the opportunity to act daringly in the selection of faculty
to teach innovative courses in Black, Afro–American, or even
Urban Studies. Old-line faculty reacted defensively to protect
their vested control of the academic domain. The very thought
of intruders with bright new approaches, especially in new fields
of instruction, posed challenges that they were not willing or
able to accept.

Among the goodies in the fall-out for the American public was
this revelation that educators were not infallible. Their judgments
as indicated by reactions of reluctance to an unexpected opportu-

nity for academic progress were shown to be, at the very least, un-imaginative. Coming at the same time as the campus rebellions by white youth, the Black student revolution leading to Black Studies programs gave substance to charges that education has become ir-relevant and unresponsive to the needs of a contemporary so-ciety. It was not surprising, in the light of the reluctance of the preservers of the academic reservation to act on their own, that students pushed even harder to select persons who met their cri-teria for competence. The University of California at Berkeley and San Francisco State experienced traumatic periods of de-structive interruptions because of abortive efforts in the interests of Eldridge Cleaver and Nathan Hare, respectively, and a few others almost as controversial. The UCLA experience of Angela Davis is a classic, unique in itself.

It was inevitable that the question of white teachers for Black Studies courses should also come up for much discussion. As usual many members of the white community, looking for opportuni-ties to malign the motives of Black students, tried various ploys to discredit their sincerity. Among the maneuvers was that of projecting as competent teachers white "scholars" who became overnight "book specialists" in various aspects of Black Studies. For the most part the attempts were presumptively ludicrous, if not actually insulting, to the Black community.

At issue is not only whether white teachers are profes-sionally competent in the usual academic terms to teach Black students. The more serious question involves moral integrity, empathetic potential, and shared notions of the way things are. Perspectives, distorted by racist-dominated insights, serve to handicap most whites in efforts to teach *any* subject to Black or white students, much less about the Black experience. What then are our answers, faced as we are with a dearth of qualified teachers of Black Studies courses?

There is, of course, the alternative of a comprehensive visiting faculty as proposed by Vincent Harding. This, however, is only a partial answer. While it is impressive, and constructive, to have a Sammy Davis, Jr., as a visiting professor of drama, a Julian Bond as a visiting professor of political science, or an Arthur

Fletcher as a visiting professor of labor economics, students need the permanent presence of less glamorous teachers who can maintain a consistent academic climate within the school.

More practical is the interweaving of a network of off-campus or visiting Black specialists with the on-campus regular faculty. By regular faculty it is not meant that the normal credentialing process should not be drastically modified. It must be.

The regular faculty in a school committed to innovation and relevance should include people of high competence who have gained their expertise in unorthodox ways—that is through experience rather than formal college courses. People such as Chester Higgins, Sr., the noted senior editor of *Jet* magazine; Renault Robinson, executive director of the Afro–American Patrolman's League; Ramsey Lewis, the distinguished musician; Fannie Lou Hamer, the fearless Mississippi freedom fighter; Jesse Jackson, the charismatic theologian; Huey Newton, the Black Panther leader; and the leaders, artists, musicians, who are part of the community served by the school; all must be considered as legitimate candidates for permanent faculty positions.

Probably most important and most often overlooked is the role that indigenous community people, mothers and fathers of students, without master's or bachelor's degrees, can play as recruiting agents, counselors, activities coordinators, and community relations specialists. Both in the public schools and the colleges these persons could be utilized to cope with shortages of competent "professionals." Incidentally, utilization of this particular reservoir of personnel could reduce materially the cost of expanding collegiate programs to create greater opportunity.

So, in reality, the question of whether white teachers can teach Black students is not the major issue. We can begin, however, by saying that on balance the answer with respect to white teachers of Black Studies courses is a qualified no—although there are some outstanding exceptions at a few institutions. Generally, however, we are talking about a variety of courses that must be taught with empathy from a Black perspective; a series of new courses involving the Black experience; and innovative courses concerned with the ultimate liberation and self-determination of the Black community. In all of this, there *is* room for the white scholar, at least certain among them. But the inescapable fact remains that most white teachers have just not had the opportunities to develop the necessary sensitivities, much less the informational background, to perform independently in Black Studies programs.

There is also serious question about the competence of far too many white teachers to teach Black students any subject. For this reason, when competent Black teachers are not available, a kind of copartnership might be feasible between noncredentialed Blacks who can establish the proper rapport and credentialed whites—or even Blacks who, themselves, have lost sensitivity.

Another practical approach to developing the needed teachers for Black students is a retraining and sensitizing of credentialed teachers so they could work more effectively with resource people who have been a part of the varied experience of Black people.

All of these suggestions are easily recognized as temporary expedients for the most part, at least as they apply to teachers of scholarly studies. One ultimate aim of Black Studies programs must be the production of competent Black people in every scholastic and technical discipline to serve as teachers, community builders, and leaders. White products of these programs will also be far superior to their present counterparts in teaching Black students in any curriculum and as leaders in their own white communities. They will be in a much more advantageous position to contribute to the elimination of racist attitudes from educational processes and programs.

To return to an earlier issue that is basic to this entire discussion, the credentialing process needs to be overhauled throughout education—eliminated if you will. For those who will cry out "standards, standards—they are destroying standards," it must be understood that the recommended overhauling is a first step toward structuring real standards—standards that are meaningful, relevant, and defensible. *Drastic modification of credentialing practices may be the first major contribution of Black Studies to the revitalizing of American education as a whole.*

To sum up, teachers for Black Studies courses are available if flexibility and resourcefulness prevail. Although in some disciplines white teachers may have the required academic competence, they are usually nevertheless not qualified to teach in Black Studies programs or to teach Black students as has been pointed out. When white teachers have the required academic competence in areas other than Black Studies, an appropriate orientation to the Black students they will be teaching, through strong guidance and Black leadership, is essential for teaching effectiveness.

W. E. B. DuBois summed up the need to get under the skin in the general area of education for the Black community when he said: "[Black] youth must be taught by [Black] and white teachers." It is simply that the latter must be *made* competent in social relations, where they are not, and rendered sensitive, where the need exists.

Education is an important element in the struggle for human rights. It is the means to help our children and people rediscover their identity and self-respect. Education is our passport to the future, for tomorrow belongs to those who prepare for it today.

Malcolm X El Hadjj El Malik Shabazz

8

THE MESSAGE AND THE HUMANISM OF MALCOLM X

Malcolm X Shabazz, born Malcolm Little, was assassinated February 21, 1965, in New York City.

The legend of his life and his message are continuing to grow in a way that represents a phenomenon of our times. The fact that his name has now become synonymous with educational excellence and renewed moral hope throughout America is no less phenomenal.

The legend of Malcolm X is a chronicle of a major part of the contemporary American scene that is unfamiliar to too many millions of white Americans.

The message of Malcolm X is primarily a message to his Black brothers and sisters; his copartners in the social scene locked in by invisible walls of prejudice, discrimination, intolerance, and race hatred. But it is also a message to the whites of the nation who still appear stunned by the emergence of the Black man as a figure of militant protest and reform.

The answer is implied in his message for all those who ask why the discontent across the nation? Why the demands for economic as well as social equality? Why are Black people seeking control of weakened Black communities rather than integration into strong white communities?

The very strength of the man—his indomitable will, his flexibility, his humanity, and his sense of purpose—is the dominant factor in his appeal to Black youth. This appeal grows stronger each day. His life, principles, hopes, and great humanity have become the inspiration for the college on Chicago's West Side that bears his name.

Malcolm X El Hadjj Malik Shabazz is for Black youth the greatest hero of modern times. Not Martin Luther King nor any other Black man acknowledged in his leadership by whites has won the admiration of Black youths as has the incomparable Black leader, known in his earlier life as "Big Red."

The story of Malcolm X is the story of the Black man in America. A one-time dope peddler, hustler, and convict lacking formal education, he learned to dramatize the condition of Black and other oppressed people. Sometimes critical, sometimes gentle, but always honest, the voice of Malcolm X painted a true picture of the Black man. His brush missed nothing as it swept across the canvas of life in America. Nonviolence, self-determination, nationhood, Pan–Africanism, the role of the Black man today, Black pride, religion for the Black man, he told all in stark realism about his people and their plight.

The white community believed that Malcolm X during his life was an irreversible Black racist committed to terroristic designs. He is still viewed by many whites in his death as a symbol of race hatred to be feared rather than respected, hated rather than admired.

Malcolm's articulate portraits of the Black-white conflict and his incisive descriptions of white exploitation of Black humanity endeared him to most Black Americans long before white America became remotely aware of his broad appeal.

Quite obviously, Blacks and whites view Malcolm X differently. One might assign the paradox represented by the contrasting white-Black views on Malcolm X to the usual plethora of such disagreements affecting most, if not all, racially different views of life in the country. But if not different in kind, this particular conflict certainly differs in degree from all others.

It seems imperative if the two groups, white and Black, are ever to find a common ground for resolution of issues of race, white America must gain insights into the man who would be the first nominee of Black youth honored with a national holiday commemorating his birth.

In his earlier life, Malcolm X was all of the things cited by white people, many of whom sighed with relief upon his assassination. In his later life, he became all of the things that have immortalized him in the minds of Black youth. The dichotomy of his life is illustrated by his statement: "In the past I made . . . sweeping indictments of all white people, the entire white race, and these generalizations have caused injuries to some whites who perhaps did not deserve to be hurt. Because of the spiritual enlightenment which I was blessed to receive as the result of my recent pilgrimage to the Holy City of Mecca, I no longer subscribe to sweeping indictments of any one race."

Another example of the spiritual struggle that contributed so much to his development, is the following: "If I can die having brought any light, having exposed any meaningful truth that will help to destroy the racist cancer that is malignant in the body of America—then, all of the credit is due to Allah. Only the mistakes have been mine."

Even Malcolm X's younger life has positive overtones for Black youth because his life was the Black experience personified.

The Autobiography of Malcolm X is fast becoming one of the most important social documents of the 20th century. Sales, still on the rise, total nearly two-million copies. Schools in every strata of society are adopting it as a textbook in such classes as English composition, social science, literature, and a variety of courses in sociology and humanism. The book is as likely to be the textbook in a freshman level high school class as in a senior level college class. It has also served as the basis for graduate studies and innumerable doctoral dissertations. No library of any note can call its collection complete without a copy of this book about a Black man who dared the wrath of Black and white America alike as he forged new concepts of human rights, and delineated the basic issues involved in a struggle for dignity, justice, and freedom all over the world.

The unbelievable impact of the book, immense as it is, pales beside the even more unbelievable impact of the man. Unbelievable, that is, when one considers the facts of life in America as they relate to a Black ex-convict labeled as a hustler, and worse, and converted as a Muslim in the Nation of Islam and ultimately to the Moslem religion.

In a ministry that lasted 12 years and for which he prepared all his life, even though unknowingly for most of it, Malcolm X created new levels of hope for millions who had come to despair man's potential for reversing a racing trend toward inhumanity and ultimate extinction.

While so many whites believed that Malcolm spoke for a few Blacks and Martin Luther King spoke for many, millions of his race were tingling before their television sets exhorting him to "give them hell" when he spoke of the effects of implacable white racism on Black people.

For the youth, Malcolm came to represent renewed manhood in a society which systematically brutalizes Black manhood. He was symbolic of an unquenchable desire for freedom. His unrelenting stance on questions of justice, equality, and freedom appealed to their fierce indignation over their frustrating condition. In his fiery alternatives, spoken often in the flaming rhetoric of potential violence, youth found reconciliation for their inherent concern with humanity, and their newly awakened belief that freedom is a right that must be "taken" if withheld— taken, as Malcolm phrased it "by any means necessary."

He was fiercely determined on this point, as his often quoted statement shows: "When you hear me say *by any means necessary* I mean exactly that. I believe in anything that is necessary to correct unjust conditions—political, economic, social, physical, anything that's necessary. I believe in it—as long as it's intelligently directed and designed to get results."

Malcolm was admired also because he was an extraordinarily clear thinker with a penchant for synthesizing political and philosophical ideas accurately and succinctly. He studied and distilled Black thought published over 100 years, and found identification with all oppressed people.

A realist of the first order, Malcolm was still a romanticist who loved people while appreciating life. Youth could sense this. Youth could also sense his identification with idealistic principles no longer prominent in the philosophies of most American leaders. Here was a deeply religious man who always maintained the symbol of his ministry while he pointed a piercing finger of accusation at racist-dominated institutions eroding the foundations of the nation's existence.

Above all, young Blacks today continue to identify with Malcolm's determined humanism. His belief that every man's right to be human is nonnegotiable confirmed the rightness of their suspicions that the yoke of their oppression was an injustice that should be thrown off even if their alternatives were reduced to violence.

The years of Malcolm's early manhood were spent in the way that most young Black men spent their time in those days and to a large extent in these days also. Malcolm spoke of these experiences in words that are universally understood, though often in different ways, by all who can or want to empathize with this period in the country's history. He was seeking and suffering while he sought. He was at the same time negotiating one of the most agonizing phases of the Black experience in America, a time when all the promise of America was revealed for whites only.

Malcolm X, like all Black Americans, was plagued by an identity confusion. His was the pursuit of an ideal that he could never fully achieve, because it required him to lose the Blackness serving as a major basis for his second-class status and become as white as circumstances and nature might allow.

This was a period in the '30s and '40s when many Black Americans were trying to do the same thing. Bleaching creams to make the skin lighter and lye-based concoctions to make

hair straighter were big sellers among a people who usually didn't
have enough money for proper food, clothing, or housing. The
reason? An unquenchable belief that to lose the "curse" of
Blackness was to open new doors of opportunity for full participation in the benefits promised by the Constitution and the Bill
of Rights.

Such an approach, as psychology tells us over and over again,
is bound to fail. It can only lead to frustration, self-degradation,
and a burning hatred spewing in all directions.

To some it may also seem strange that most Black youth chose
Malcolm as a "messiah" without choosing the religion that he selected as his own. Rejecting Christianity because of its intimate
involvement with every stage of their suffering, they have not,
for the most part, accepted the religious alternative that apparently contributed so much to the spiritual reclamation of their
new hero.

Resolution of this issue may still be long in coming. On the
other hand it may be that Malcolm himself, together with his
creed and his beliefs, is the spiritual foundation upon which a
new religion is already being built. Time will tell. In any
event, contributing to a resurrection of basic human values in a
way that few recognized initially, this man has begun now to
emerge as one of the greatest humanists the world has ever
known. Even now there are those who speak of him with the
same reverence accorded Christianity's Jesus Christ.

The mystery of how this all came about is intertwined in a
complex way with the many paradoxes and contradictions that
have been a part of this country's history from its beginning.

The start of this saga of destiny was the birth of Malcolm X,
ironically, in the State of Nebraska where matters of race have
been viewed historically as the opposite of conditions in Mississippi.

In his autobiography, Malcolm describes days just before his
birth when members of the Ku Klux Klan of Omaha descended
upon his father's home threatening to do him bodily harm if he
did not cease "stirring up" the local "Negroes."

His father was ultimately killed in Lansing, Michigan, by the notorious Black Legion, a white terrorist organization similar to the KKK.

The autobiography also describes an early youth of turmoil and struggle:

> My mother . . . seemed to be always working—cooking, washing, ironing, cleaning, and fussing over us eight children. . . . My father's skull . . . was crushed in. . . . His body was cut almost in half. . . . I was six . . . there were times when we would be so hungry we were dizzy . . . when I began to get caught stealing . . . she [my mother] would whip me. . . . my mother suffered a complete breakdown [and] remained in the same [mental] hospital for twenty-six years. . . . I wasn't really surprised when I was expelled [from school]. . . . my English teacher . . . said . . . you've got to be realistic about being a nigger . . . why don't you plan on carpentry [not law]. . . . I worked washing dishes.

Part of his later youth was spent in Roxbury, Massachusetts in relative affluence (for Black people, that is), but without relief from the psychological confusion inspired by the profusion of contradictions one finds in any Black community.

"I saw those Roxbury Negroes acting and living differently from any Black people I'd ever seen in my life. . . . I thought I was seeing . . . high-class, educated, important Negroes."

Reflecting later on this he concluded that: "What I was really seeing was only a big-city version of those successful Negro bootblacks and janitors back in Lansing." He viewed these persons as part of the syndrome where Black people were supposed to strive with all in them to become the biggest and most important "inferior" people in town. "The truth was that eight out of ten of the Hill Negroes of Roxbury, despite the impressive-sounding job titles they affected, actually worked as menials and servants," Malcolm said.

As a shoeshine boy, dancer, hustler, and gambler, Malcolm lived his way through the streets of Boston and later, Harlem. His description of the experiences of those days creates a twinge of nostalgia on the part of thousands of Black readers who lived in the same way at the same time and do to this day. The painful reality of what he said brings back memories to many readers with such sharp abruptness that it feels as if a knife is being plunged into the very insides of one's soul. It is not unusual for a Black reader to feel sorrow, hatred, anxiety, or fear as life in the Black ghetto is depicted in all of its garish reality.

The humor and pathos, sustaining factors in Black survival, are also in his book—in the people—"Cadillac Drake," "Sammy the Pimp," "Dollar-bill" and his "Kansas City Roll," "Few-clothes" the pickpocket, "Jumpsteady" the burglar, "Creole Bill," and "Chicago Red" [Redd Foxx].

In a startling way, the book is the life of all Black people as well as the life of an individual man.

Malcolm's life as a Black youth in a major urban center led eventually to a 10-year sentence at the Charlestown prison in Massachusetts.

As the autobiography points out, life in prison started out to be simply an extension of life in the streets. But he overcame temptations of a prison with more evils than the streets and turned instead to a library for knowledge.

His understandable rage began to settle into a more calculating pattern. Undergirding the struggling rebirth of a soul in torment was a searching need for a spiritual foundation on which a philosophy of life could be constructed. This need was fulfilled shortly after his transfer to Concord prison by his conversion to the Nation of Islam as a follower of the Honorable Elijah Muhammad. He was converted to the orthodox Islam religion before his death.

Despite the persecution by prison officials growing out of their negative attitude toward Muslims, Malcolm persevered both in the study of his new religion and in the quest for knowledge.

In addition to his voracious reading in prison, Malcolm began to demonstrate his talent as a leader of men. Instructors who taught at the prison from such prestigious schools as Boston University and Harvard University found him also a formidable opponent in debates on a variety of issues, especially those involving race, racism, exploitation, and injustice. They marveled at the response of other prisoners to Malcolm's exhortations.

During his studies in prison, he became more convinced that

endless contradictions existed between what America claimed to be and what it actually was in terms of the treatment accorded its colored and racial minorities. He also concluded that much of the most popular reading material about life in America was based on hypocrisy and outright falsehoods.

He saw with a revealing clarity the difference between segregation and separation. Segregation he described as a condition of life forced upon a people, regulated from the outside. Separation was described as a condition entered into voluntarily by two equals for the good of both.

The penetrating insights of Malcolm, steeped as they were in bitterness, were revealed in the statement that, "All of us who might have probed space, or cured cancer, or built industries were, instead, Black victims of the white man's American social system."

He noted that instead of social contributions that would build humanity, we have a situation where in "every big city ghetto tens of thousands of yesterday's and today's school dropouts are keeping body and soul together by some form of hustling."

Malcolm gave to Black youth a description that would have been both apt and appreciated by this writer at the age of 16 years: "Hustler, uneducated, unskilled at anything honorable, but nervy and cunning enough to live by wits, exploiting every prey."

Even while in prison, Malcolm spoke of how Black people were taught to be ashamed of their Blackness, and how their shame led them to become instruments of their own victimization in an almost unbelievable variety of ways. His understanding of how the success image for Black people was always a white ideal, made white listeners writhe then as later when he articulated this understanding in the quiet but firm language of a man who had begun to transcend the destiny originally conceived for him.

Malcolm devised a learning style in prison that was uniquely suited for an intelligent being deprived of some of the learning tools considered indispensable for success in the usual traditional settings. He virtually devoured a collegiate level dictionary. He

would read aloud from his own writing until the page was memorized. The iron-willed discipline is obvious. In prison he developed for himself the equivalent of a college education with a
major in humanities.

Malcolm was released on parole, August 9, 1952, to begin his
actual ministry of Black liberation. This was a mission of humanitarian fulfillment, undertaken with a sense of zealous commitment that could erupt only from a deeply religious base.

The guiding precepts of his new life were basic to his continued development as a model for the new kind of Black man
he hoped to create in liberating the old kind of Negro from his
"slave mentality." He believed that "Heaven and hell were conditions of life endured by people right here on earth; the Black
man will never get respect until he learns to respect his woman;
freedom, justice, and equality will come about for Black people
when they become willing to pay any price necessary to get them;
Black people must turn their backs on tobacco, liquor, narcotics,
dancing, gambling, movies, lying, stealing, and domestic quar-
reling."

His enthusiastic dedication was tempered by the knowledge
that, "no true leader burdens his following with a greater load
than they can carry, and no true leader sets too fast a pace for
his followers to keep up."

Malcolm believed that one of the white man's tricks was to
keep the Black race divided and fighting each other. "This has
traditionally kept Black people from achieving the unity which
was the worst need of the Black race in America," he said. His
autobiography documents the extent of America's failure in the
area of Black-white relations as he saw it: "The Western world's
most learned diplomats have failed to solve this grave race problem. Her learned legal experts have failed. Her sociologists have
failed. Her civil leaders have failed. Her fraternal leaders have
failed."

The way that white America viewed the nation of Islam
(Black Muslims) did much to thrust Malcolm into the spotlight
as he expounded his scathing indictment of America for her

failure to eliminate racism as a national characteristic. He was under constant surveillance.

His incomprehensibility for white critics was an extension of the lack of information by most whites about Black America's people. "I would hate to be general of an army as badly informed as the American white man has been about the Negro," he said.

Travel abroad did much to modify Malcolm's perspective on race and human conflict. Through trips all over Africa and the Moslem world, he developed a new outlook on the colonialistic existence of Black Americans. He came to see that the condition of Black people was closely related to the plight of other have-nots—the browns, the reds, and even poor whites. His plea became an orchestration on the rights of man.

It was Malcolm who helped Black youth understand that revolution must take place in oneself before he can function correctly to help others. Youth learned that the truly revolutionary struggle is not based on strategy and tactics alone, but on truth. "It is from truth and truth alone that Black youth must operate. That must be his base; his motive for struggle; his will to survive."

Malcolm was saying essentially that leadership involves responsibility for being a man renewed in spirit, mind, and body. "A man must inspire people and his actions must give a glimpse of what lies ahead. He gives clear direction in work, deed, and in his very being. He is patient, considerate, helpful, compassionate, strong and uncompromising."

Applying all of his powers of analysis to education for the masses, Malcolm concluded that the educational process should unleash a sense of inner power and a recognition of the requirements for group power. Education should empower, not de-power.

Selected courses are important only as they are related to reality. The content should flow from the Black experience and

"—from the pragmatic to the theoretical—"
"—from the informal to the formal—"
"—from Black awareness to Black relevant competence—"

"—from teacher sources to student sources—"

"—from group education to self-education—"

"—from the acquisition of basic skills to the application of these skills to real life problems—"

"—from the individual acquisition of ability to the utilization of this new-found ability in the cause of collective Black survival—"

"—from understanding one's membership within the Black nation to the application of one's brain power to the strengthening of that nation's ability to survive—to resist exploitation and to implement its own stated intentions—"

It is the interrelationship of various courses to each other and to real life which makes them relevant. An important key is the student's role in educating himself to learn to love learning for the benefit of his own people. Malcolm believed this and also held the following to be true.

Africanization should pervade the entire educational experience in descriptive, analytical, historical and intellectual terms. The spiritual and human qualities of the experience and the search for a relevant set of values cannot be separated from this process. There is no such thing as a value-free course of curriculum. The Black Experience is *intra*curricular; nothing which affects Black people should be *extra*curricular.

The education of Black people should be controlled and developed and shaped by the Black consensus wherever Black people are being educated. We must stop the massive educational assembly-line production of the "made-in-America Negroes."

A massive educational program should be undertaken at the street corner, doorstep, church pew, and barroom level to stimulate the engagement of a psychological and political confrontation to take over the schools in Black communities.

A national communications network should be established to promote intercity communications—the exchange of information, request for support and as a tool for undertaking nationwide action. A system should be developed to ensure that all federal funds, textbooks, consultancies, etc., that flow into the

Black community are controlled by and benefit the local community in educational, economic, and technical terms.

Malcolm's philosophy on education also encompassed the following understandings about the Black community:

> *Black awareness* for the Black community should not be misconstrued as any more than the first step toward returning "home." The nation must be built—psychologically and operationally.

> *Black precipitated crises* serve to heighten awareness to produce the confrontation out of which change becomes possible, and to provide data on which to base the future struggles.

> Think in terms of *the struggle* and not just about winning it. Struggle, in itself, will produce its own victories. Preoccupation with winning may prejudice one against the right to make honest, or even stupid, mistakes. One also learns from mistakes.

> *Demonstrate* to the Black community how the existing system has deliberately succeeded in failing to educate Black students. Use test scores, dropout and unemployment rates, the disproportionate number of Blacks who served in Vietnam, etc. Either one accepts that it has been a deliberate design not to educate Black students or he must accept that Blacks are inferior in native intelligence. Any man worth a grain of salt knows that Black is beautiful, i.e., that no man is better than any other man just because he is white. If a Black man thinks that he is inferior to anyone, it is only because he has accepted someone else's definition of himself and not really his own deeply concealed knowledge that he is in fact as good as anyone else.

> *Mobilize and organize* the Black community to think, feel, and behave consciously Black. Help brothers and sisters to ask one another how to become Black; *avoid telling* brothers and sisters to be Black. They are already aware of their Blackness; they merely fail to comprehend its positive aspects.

> *Apply legal strategies* as harassment and publicity maneuvers as well as a protection of individual rights. Do not rely excessively on the prospect of winning, but don't reject the victories.

It is not necessary to wait until a *majority* of the Black community is involved. An effective minority may be much more indicative of *what will be*; the majority is usually a reflection of *what used to be*. As you take action, also organize—organizations can flow and flower out of the action, if consciously planned.

Attempt to *cultivate student power* which communicates easily with other segments of the community.

Draw upon the resources of Blacks who work inside the system as sources of information and as advocates within the system.

In addition to the above principles as a renewed basis for racial unity, community control of schools was defined by Malcolm as the power to make and enforce decisions in certain specific areas:

Expenditure of funds—local, state and federal

Hiring and firing of all staff—including training and reprogramming

Site selection and naming of schools

Design and construction of schools—awarding and supervising of contracts

Purchasing power—for books, supplies, equipment, food services, etc.

Setting up of educational policy and programs

Merit pay to staff—increments and salary based on effective performance alone.

The composition of the governing boards of Black-controlled schools, he believed, should involve parents, students, community leaders, and teachers—of the authentically Black variety.

An effort should be made to prevent unions—white or Negro —from negotiating educational policies without the equal participation of Black community representatives. Locally controlled districts of the school might negotiate with the union on parts of the contract; the central agency with equal participation from locally controlled units might negotiate those parts of the contract (excluding salaries) which are appropriate at that level.

Aside from the idea of community control of schools as they currently exist, there is a need to examine parallel systems, operating outside of the public system, because of the system's general bankruptcy as it relates to the Black student. Such a (parallel) system would include private schools, the University of Islam, Afro–American Culture Centers, Liberation Schools, etc. These kinds of schools could serve to convince the Black community of the essential educability of its youth, to experiment with new techniques, to provide local residents with meaningful revolutionary roles, to deepen and expand the supply of effective Black talent, and to increase the possibility that the more frequently overlooked youth are provided with opportunities to increase their inputs to the movement.

Parallel systems should focus on Black history, blackening the curriculum (viewing economic, political, psychological, cultural, historical, sociological, and intellectual aspects as one interrelated body of knowledge), improving basic skills, increasing parental concern and involvement, becoming self-financing, becoming accountable to the Black community, hiring sensitive staff and relating their efforts *relevantly* to the accrediting and credentialing systems.

The curriculum of a parallel system must proceed from the position that the Black child is human and educable, with creative capabilities and potential. It must inculcate a desire to contribute toward Black nationhood and to incorporate an ability to think for one's self. It must be a process of becoming able, as one acquires the basic skills, to learn *how* to make a contribution and *which* contribution he wants to make.

This ideal system, formulating in Malcolm's mind as he conceived the Organization of Afro–American unity, sees the transmission of knowledge as inseparable from the idea of respect and mutuality: The teacher learns as he teaches; a student teaches his teachers and his classmates as he learns. The student learns as a member of a group, not solely as an individual. Each student is unique but at the same time a member of a group.

Similarly the development of people is not the exclusive domain of the formal school. Learning takes place inside and outside of the classroom. One learns from friends, from parents, and from other "significant" adults in one's life. The community is the classroom. In a bedroom or a playground, one learns as he functions and hopefully has fun as he learns.

With respect to the Black child, he is called upon to incorporate a desire to survive creatively and to acquire the tools of scholarship and to promote them as a component part of his Blackness—his consciousness of it; his skill in determining his own destiny; his desire to sustain and to cultivate his own creativity.

Stated most succinctly, it was Malcolm's position that education must be viewed as a system having definite goals and values. Its prime function was viewed as instilling in students the positive values, ideology, and vision of the system of which they are a part, with a view toward the perpetuation of that particular system. Thus education is seen as far more than merely the teaching of reading, writing, and arithmetic.

Education for Black children and youth as based on these concepts of education and life does not, in consequence, exist in a vacuum. It is an experience in humanism and survival for purposes of supporting the needs, the hopes and the dreams of a society.

The college named for him is patterned after the man, Malcolm, his ideals, and his confirmed belief in the inherent nobility of all humanity.

Students educated under this philosophy are directed toward three major goals: freedom, individuality, and service.

Freedom in a very general sense refers to a freedom from external constraints. Malcolm X College is characterized by free access to the resources of the institution, the city, the world. The role of staff and student body is to remove the obstacles which block the path of those seeking the more specific freedom defined as "the capability to deal creatively and effectively with one's situation." Malcolm X College takes the position that in order to achieve positive freedom, students must be encouraged to actively and consciously attempt to utilize their personal resources, their life style, and their experiential background in the classroom. The student must become skilled at identifying needs, problems and issues which affect the nature and quality of life in his environment and then use them in his research. Hopefully, he will learn to relate his learning to the problems of his community as well as his own.

Individuality, the College realizes, cannot genuinely exist without the freedom described above. The thrust of this perspective is to resist any simple accounts of what a person "really" is or intends to become, and to allow for distinction of one's real self; this perspective is, in our judgment, dynamic and expanding and defies prima facie, or merely quantitative assessment. Individuality presupposes a social context and, yet, underscores the uniqueness of each person in that context. It is characterized by built-in capacities (not necessarily apparent) for good which are inseparable from the good of the community and ultimately of all mankind.

Service involves being a contributing member of society by bringing one's unique resources to bear upon human problems, particularly the problems confronting the Black community. As with the others, this concept recognizes that the truly educated man is also a learned man: but more than that, he is one in whom learning is combined with an understanding of social injustice and a commitment to correcting it.

This was the message of Malcolm X El Hadjj Malik Shabazz —his endowment to his children and to all future generations of children all over this world.

BLACK NATIONAL ANTHEM
LIFT EV'RY VOICE AND SING

Lyrics by James Weldon Johnson

Lift every voice and sing, till earth and heaven ring,
Ring with the harmony of liberty.
Let our rejoicing rise, high as the list-'ning skies,
Let it resound loud as the rolling sea.
Sing a song full of the faith that the dark past has taught us;
Sing a song full of the hope that the present has brought us;
Facing the rising sun of our new day begun
Let us march on till victory is won.

Stony the road we trod, bitter the chast-'ning rod,
Felt in the days when hope unborn had died;
Yet with a steady beat, have not our weary feet
Come to the place for which our fathers sighed
We have come over a way that with tears has been watered;
We have come, treading our path thro' the blood of the
slaughtered,
Out from the gloomy past, till now we stand last
Where the white gleam of our bright star is cast.

God of our weary years, God of our silent tears,
Thou who has brought us thus far on the way;
Thou who hast by thy might, led us into the light
Keep us forever in the path, we pray.—
Lest our feet stray from the places our God, where we met
Thee.
Lest our hearts, drunk with the wine of the world, we forget
———Thee;
Shadowed beneath Thy hand, may we forever stand
True to our God, True to our native land.

APPENDIXES

Of the appendixes included in this work, the first is a strong "Report of the Workshop on Education" which was held in 1968 at the National Black Power Conference. Its content dramatically supports much that has been written in the main part of *Passport to Freedom*: the imperative need for the direct and, when necessary, the revolutionary participation by the entire Black community in its school system.

The second appendix is the recommendations made to the American Association of Junior Colleges to enable it to meet head-on the need for Black Studies programs for both Black students and white to eliminate racism in our institutions of education.

The remaining appendixes are directly related to Malcolm X College. These appendixes are not intended to be prototypes for the community college but rather represent the means by which one college is attacking the critical problem of educating Black youth to become leaders and active members of their Black communities and of their nation.

APPENDIX A

The following is a: *Report of the Workshop on Education* at the National Black Power Conference, Black Self-Learning Section, held in Philadelphia, Pennsylvania 1968, and edited by Nathan Hare, Chairman.

Whereas, Black people know more about their needs than anybody else;

Whereas, schools in Black communities controlled by whites have failed to provide the kind of education Black children need;

Whereas, the entire system of education has militated against Black persons;

Whereas, there is a vital need to rehabilitate and salvage the battered egos, white-washed soul, spirit and culture of many of our Black citizenry;

WE RESOLVE TO:

Move immediately to effect total Black control of hiring, firing, retention and promotion of all Black school personnel.

Develop coalitions among diverse Black groups to promote responsibility to the Black community.

Develop specific strategies for physically taking over schools and classrooms, disrupting racist learning, whenever the situation demands.

Develop techniques for redirecting and guiding Black professionals to take responsible stances which are consistent with the aims and goals of the Black community.

(Black control of school necessitates Black control over all school personnel.

Black "experts" must be accountable to the Black community and able to give schools the service they have given the power structure in the past.)

Demand the waiver of tests standardized on white middle-class urban experiences or give equal weight to the Black experience.

Go into the community and find out how the citizens view their schools and, in turn, assist them in evaluating the relevance and irrelevance of the schools to their lives.

Secure data with which to confront those brothers and sisters (and other relatives) who are unsympathetic to the Black interest.

Find ways to organize parents so they will know what is happening to their children.

Explain and illustrate to the community how the schools are not fulfilling their obligation to Black children and the Black community.

Begin to differentiate between such concepts as tokenism and total victory, reform and revolution, nationalism and assimilationism.

(Corps of Black revolutionaries should be constantly evaluating and reassessing the Black community.

Each local Black community should have a Black information and clearing house.

The community should demand teacher orientations conducted by the Black community.)

Establish Black nurseries and preschool studies for Black children.

Disregard the George Washington birthday holiday and replace it with a Black Winter Break, beginning with February 21st, the commemoration of the death of Malcolm X, and ending with February 23rd, the birthday of W. E. B. DuBois, the late Black scholar.

Establish Black cultural centers in each locality.

Establish Black libraries and mobile Black library units in each neighborhood.

Infiltrate the Sunday Schools as a part of the effort to rejuvenate the Black child's soul, spirit and personality.

Assist in the formation and strengthening of Black parents councils in each locality, region and neighborhood.

Form textbook evaluation corps for criticism and production of books relevant to the Black condition.

Extend "Negro History Week" the year-round and replace it with a "White History Week" for a special week's concentration on the study and exposure of the science of white racism and its history. (This also is a year-round concern.)

Establish Black scholarly and academic journals.

Provide conferences to educate those Brothers and Sisters who express curiosity about the meaning of Blackness, Black power and the like.

Work toward redefining all pertinent values and standards toward building a Black morality relevant to the Black reality.

Establish a "captive action" week commemorating the day our Black forefathers were abducted and transported in chains to the abominable American colonialists.

(Every Black person who knows something must find one or two Black Brothers and Sisters to teach.)

Require that all teachers in Black schools undergo a year's in-service de-brainwashing program administered by the Black community.

Revive the national anthem, "Lift Every Voice and Sing," to replace the singing of the "Star Spangled Banner" in morning devotional exercises in Black schools.

Develop techniques for converting colleges and institutions now Black in name and color composition only into true Black institutions.

Continue efforts to build Black universities.

Organize intelligence squads to infiltrate each educational institution, white or "Negro."

Assist in the establishment of a Black or Afro-American student union on each high school, junior high and college campus.

Assist in the establishment of a Black Studies or Afro-American Studies curriculum at each institution.

Continue to promote the establishment of several model Black universities.

APPENDIX B

Black Caucus Recommendations to the American Association of Junior Colleges

1. *1972 Conference Theme*
   The theme should reflect upon the manifestations of racism and its possible solutions, such as:

    a. Student body composition compared to eligible Black student population
    b. Racial balance in staff
    c. Provisions for staff upgrading and training
    d. Legitimizing of Black Studies and integration of them into the regular curriculum.

AAJC should seriously consider recommending mandatory Black Studies for all students as a part of general education.

2. *Advocacy*
   The Association should assume a strong advocacy position concerning programs and activities that affect the providing of higher education to Black students. These include:

a. Endorsing the concept of community control through broader Black participation in decision-making, other than that presently represented by Trustee members

b. Support of critical supportive services such as day care and financial aid

c. Endorsing sanctions of institutions found to be guilty of discrimination of any kind in providing services, hiring, contracts, etc.

d. Developing sensitivity to needs of Black students wherever they are found

e. Support of increased Black participation on Joint Apprenticeship Councils

f. Support of increased Upward Bound participation for junior colleges.

3. Review of Dr. Gleazer's Report*

A Black task force should be convened to review with Dr. Gleazer the findings of his *Project Focus* before the first draft is prepared, since we doubt that he has had the kind of major exposure to Black students, Black staff, or Black community needs that is necessary.

4. Staff and organizational representation

We recommend that the professional and office staff of the Association reflect the percentage of Black students in community and junior colleges across the country, and that attempts be made to employ Blacks in regular full-time staff positions not depending on special project grants.

5. Junior College Journal

a. Special issue should be planned on the education of Black students in community colleges.

b. Black perspectives should be given on all major topics covered in depth by the Journal.

c. A monthly Black column should be initiated.

6. Regional Workshops

More emphasis should be placed upon regional workshops dealing

---

*Dr. Edmund Gleazer is Executive Director of AAJC on leave at time of publication of this book to perform in-depth analyses of community colleges in the United States.

with Black concerns in junior college programs, with local determination of the subject matter of the workshops, assisted by technical assistance from the AAJC staff. Participation in these workshops should not be limited to Black staff.

7. *Black organization within AAJC*
   a. We recommend that AAJC formally recognize a Black affiliate to be made up of administrators, faculty, trustees, and students representing member institutions.
   b. Provisions should be made to facilitate regional meetings of such an organization as well as for implementing a communication mechanism to reach Black representatives in all segments found at the campus level.

8. *Needs of private Black colleges*
   The Association should give special attention to providing technical assistance and legislative focus upon the needs of the 17 or so small Black private junior colleges, in order for them to survive and become viable, accredited institutions.

9. *Exhibit structure and staffing at regional meeting*
   a. More sensitivity should be used in planning exhibit materials. (Example: The Polaroid exhibit on South African Passports was offensive to most of us.)
   b. An attempt should be made to recruit Black firms to offer exhibits.
   c. A greater effort should be made to have Black staff manning exhibits.

Note: These recommendations reflect some current concerns and attitudes of Black educators in a rather forceful way. Similarities should be observed between these points and those more specifically stated in *The Report of the Black Power Conference* of 1968.

APPENDIX C

Symbols, Reality at Malcolm X
by L. E. Palmer, Jr.

Symbolism blended with reality last week when the new home of an extraordinarily important educational institution was dedicated.

The symbolism was breathtaking. A huge crowd of blacks stood at attention in front of Malcolm X College, arms upraised, fists clenched, all eyes on the flag post.

Already fluttering in the breeze were the Stars and Stripes and the flag of the State of Illinois. Inching up a third flag pole was the flag of the Black Nation.

It dropped limp against the pole as it was eased toward the top, but when it finally was jerked into position, the flag of the Black Nation unfurled in its tri-color glory.

At that very instant a 21-gun salute boomed through the dreary West Side area where the $26 million building stands as an oasis in a desert of despair.

For the first time, the flag of the Black Nation flies over a public building in the United States.

The flag, with three horizontal bars, is described by Edward Vaughn of the Pan American Congress:

"The top red is for the blood all black people have shed and must continue to shed in order to achieve the Black Nation.

"The second bar is black, representing our race. Our civilization predates all others and although we have fallen on evil days, we will rise again to take our rightful place in the world.

"The third bar is green, symbolic of land and nationhood. No people can be truly free unless they have a land base. Land is the basis of power and freedom. The black flag means black nationalism and black nationalism means land and power."

This symbolism will not be lost on the black students who will see the black flag flying in the breeze above Malcolm X college as they enter this new structure, which houses one of the most revolutionary approaches to education in the nation.

This bold new effort at bringing relevancy to blacks in college is the reality that awaited students participating in the dedication of Malcolm X College.

Dr. Charles G. Hurst, the little dynamo of a man who is president of this unusual college, looked at the new, long, modern structure and said:

"This building is the instrument by which we begin the process of liberating our community. I dedicate this institution to the community, to all black people and all people who support the black cause."

The dedication of Malcolm X college in its new quarters came three days before the May 19th birthday of Malcolm X Shabazz-El Hajj Malik El Shabazz who was assassinated Feb. 21, 1965.

No greater tribute could ever be given to this extraordinary man, who rose from the ranks of pimp, hustler, and convict to become the black shining prince, the idol of black youths.

In the light of where Brother Malcolm came from, what heights he reached, how he articulated, led, and provided an untarnished image for downtrodden black malehood, a revolutionary college bearing his name is the perfect monument to his memory.

Relevant education was seen by Malcolm X as a key factor in the liberation of the black man's mind. He contended that through positive, black-oriented and black-directed channels of education, the black man could free himself to take other steps toward the development of real institutions of power that would enable him to secure his place in this universe.

Reprinted with permission from *The Chicago Daily News*, May 22-23, 1971.

APPENDIX D

Some Courses and Curricula at Malcolm X College

Political Science 202: Urban Government and Politics
Political Science 208: Seminar in Power Politics
Political Science 211: Analysis of White Racism
Political Science 212: Principles of Community Politics
Political Science 215: Politics of Community Organization

Sociology 202: Sociology of Urban Life
Sociology 206: Juvenile Delinquency
Sociology 213: Sociology of the Black Family

Communications Media 151: Black Journalism

Art 130: Afro–American Art

Literature 121: Contemporary Afro–American Literature
Literature 122: Perspectives in Black Literature
Literature 123: Slave Narratives
Literature 125: Psychology in Black Literature

Literature 131: Survey of Afro–American Poetry

Fine Arts 106: African Tribal Arts

Swahili 101-104

Music 131: Black Music Wokshop
Music 200: Black Music Workshop
Music 208: Gospel Arts and Artists

Physical Education 109: Afro–Cuban and Primitive Dance

Anthropology 204: Culture of Sub–Sahara Africa
Anthropology 220: Theatre of Black Life in America

Education 150: Black Education

History 114: The Afro–American in American History
History 115: Afro–American History Since 1865
History 119: History of the Black Theatre
History 247: African History to Colonial Period

Political Science 210: Principles of Political Economy

Sociology 241: Institutional Racism

APPENDIX E

Institutional Racism
(Abbreviated Course Outline)

Introduction and Purpose

Racism, conscious and unconscious, so permeates every aspect of life in America that no segment can remain unaffected. Over the years racism has become literally metabolized in the bloodstream of the society directing the actions and thinking of individuals and corporations, alike.

Individual racism is vicious and sometimes deadly. But most invidious is the institutionalized racism observable in all of our important institutions. Serving as the guarantor of its own perpetuation, institutional racism becomes the single most dangerous threat to this country's existence as a free nation. Yet it is so little understood by even our most educated persons. The principal aim of this course is to fill this relative void for those seeking answers to racial unrest, increasing racial polarities, and liberation for all oppressed people.

Major Areas of Study

1. Overview of racial attitudes and injustices in America
2. Racism in education from kindergarten through college.

3. Racism in law and public service agencies
4. Racism in government and politics
5. Racism in health care and education
6. Racism in urban life: employment, housing, etc.
7. Racism in religion
8. Review, analysis, synthesis, and conclusions.

Evaluation

Each major area of study is followed by a quiz with a midterm coming after Section 4, Racism in Government and Politics. All quizzes and examinations are essay-type, with make-ups permitted under only the most extenuating conditions. The final examination follows an open-book format since it is the student's critical insights, understandings, and ability to analyze that represents the major objective of the course. An average of 80 is required on all quizzes and examinations.

All students are required to:

1. Maintain a file of clippings from newspapers, periodicals, etc., submitting copies regularly for inspection and return.

2. Complete an essay on each section from any desired point of view.

3. Read at least six books from the bibliography or approved substitutes. (He must also read the Autobiography of Malcolm X if he has not done so.) Recommended for all are the writings of Frantz Fanon. Book reports on these latter will earn varying amounts of extra credit.

4. Students must read, analyze, and be prepared to comment upon the variety of auxiliary materials distributed in class.

5. Each student must present a critical review of the 60 minute film: "A Rap Session witht Dr. Hurst and Black Youth."

6. Each student must complete a term paper of appropriate length, properly documented, organized, etc. on a topic under one of the major headings listed above. The student may also conduct his research in the areas of communications media, business and industry, or labor unions.

7. Familiarity with the special resource materials available for further study after completing the course is required, (Journal of Black Studies, Black Lines, etc.).

8. At least one major field trip to a prison or other social problem center must be completed and reported upon in writing.

Students must meet individually with the teacher at least once each semester. Each student is also required to enroll in the Learning Center.

Institutional Racism
Quiz

1. Define Institutional Racism in your own terms.

2. Describe three acts of Institutional Racism that happens regularly in this city.

3. Describe difference between individual white racism and institutional racism.

4. Give three (3) examples of white racism that occur regularly.

5. Define nationalism in your own words and discuss the various forms of Nationalism as they were described in class.

6. Tell me something about yourself in relation to the problems stated above. What do you feel is your course of action to make your community and the world a better place to live?

APPENDIX F

Some Special Programs at Malcolm X College

Urban Studies

The Urban Studies Institute offers curricula that are constructed to develop leadership in the urban community. Our nation's urban communities are no longer white, they are multiracial. Members of ethnic groups which have recently arrived on the urban scene of America must be educated in this leadership.

The Urban Studies Institute offers fields of specialization in the following:

Metropolitan Studies
Urban Planning
Police Science
Social Service Administration.

In addition to curricula development, the Urban Studies Institute cooperates with Malcolm X College's Department of Community Services and Continuing Education. Seminars in Narcotics and Dangerous Drugs, Crime and Delinquency, and the City in Crisis are being jointly planned. The Urban Studies Institute provides teaching staff for such programs as the Parolee Assistance Program, the Prison Annex and the Independent Studies Program.

Adult and Continuing Education

Malcolm X College's programs of adult and continuing education have the potential to lead a constructive revolution in the advancement of minority groups. Conscientiously developed programs of Adult and Continuing Education are uniquely situated to replace the vacuum created by traditional education with solid, useful learning. Included in this program are:

Classes and short courses which are regularly scheduled meetings of formally organized groups on campus and in the community. These courses are not tied to the college's time schedule.

Conferences, institutes and/or workshops
Seminars
Lecture series
Discussion groups
Closed circuit audio and TV instruction.

The Black Police Academy

In order to improve the quality of police service, Malcolm X College has established the Black Police Academy. Each semester, thirty (30) Black students, interested in police work as a career, will be enrolled as Cadets in the Academy. This Academy is not affiliated with any municipal or state police department.

Past curricula in Police Science and Justice Administration have vainly attempted to avert the polarization and alienation that is presently taking place in our cities. The reality is that our police and justice authorities are part of the very cement that hold this society together. As such, their training must at all times be effective.

Health Facilities Management Program

This program, leading to the Associate of Arts Degree, consists of regular college courses to be taken on campus in combination with clinical Health Facilities Management courses to be conducted at affiliated hospitals. This program requires two academic years. Admission to the program is based on meeting the entrance requirements of the college.

The School of Nursing

Nursing careers are available for both men and women. Foundations of nursing, care of mothers and babies, and the care of physically and mentally ill adults and children are among the courses taught.

The nursing program is approved by the Committee of Nurse Examiners, Department of Registration and Education of the State of Illinois, has reasonable assurance of accreditation from the National League for Nursing, and is approved by the Office of the Superintendent of Public Instruction for the State of Illinois.

Hospitals, clinics, nursing homes, and doctor's offices are only some of the challenging settings where registered nurses are needed.

Cooperative Mid-Management Development

This is a two-year program leading to an Associate of Arts Degree. The program is designed to prepare students for employment at the middle-management level in the fields of marketing, distribution and retailing. The program has two options: (1) attending classes during the day and working after school; (2) work-experience and instruction arranged so that students alternately attend college full time for one semester and then practice what they have learned in addition. Students will be paid by their employers for their on-the-job experience.

Accounting and Computing

A two-year semiprofessional program intended to prepare students for responsible positions in accounting in business, industry, and government agencies. The program also meets the needs of individuals now employed who require additional training in accounting for advancement.

Business Administration

A two-year program intended to lay the foundation for responsible positions in business and industry. Graduates will be prepared for entry positions in business management, office management, purchasing, sales and related areas requiring a broad and integrated knowledge of business operations and techniques.

Commercial Art and Advertising Display

This two-year professional program is designed to provide the necessary training and basic skills needed to prepare students for a challenging and rewarding career in Commercial Art and Advertising

Display. Students learn from highly skilled, professional instructors, and will receive some experience in an on-the-job cooperative work-study program. Curriculum includes communication skills, related mathematics, business education, art and other electives. Graduates will receive Associate in Applied Science Degrees.

Cooperative Business Work-Study Programs

In addition to the Cooperative Mid-Management Program, students majoring in Business Administration may become involved in the Cooperative Business Work-Study Programs. In this program, students may receive up to a total of 35 hours credit, while working full time. The actual number of hours received will be determined by the type and nature of their work-study experience.

Engineering and Related Technology Programs

These two-year professional programs are designed to provide students with a strong, well-balanced curriculum in engineering and related technologies, including related science, mathematics and general education. Graduates receive Associate in Applied Science Degrees in the following options:

>   Architecture
>   Engineering
>   Civil Technology (Structural and Highway options)
>   Drafting
>   Industrial Design.

The two-year curriculum includes a thorough study of the materials and processes used in the above areas as well as emphasis on a specialized area. Communications skills which teach the student to interpret, analyze, and transmit facts and ideas graphically, orally, and in writing are also a part of the curriculum.

This technology training prepares students for employment in industry at the technical level.

Graphic Arts

This program provides the necessary training and basic skills needed to prepare a student for a career in Graphic Arts.

Emphasis is given to principles, techniques and fundamental skills in offset printing, composition, photography, plate-making, collating, binding, cutting and layout.

Plant Engineering

The objective of the program is to prepare students for employment as building managers, custodial supervisors, maintenance supervisors, and building operating technicians in the occupational areas of business, industry, and government. Academic and technical exposure will provide a well-balanced learning experience designed to equip the candidate with the necessary skills to function successfully in the field of Building Management.

Project Impact

Project Impact is a 26-week training program which develops entrance-level skills through the use of exploratory workshops in four general areas: drafting, metal, wood, and electricity. A component of G.E.D. is included in the program for students who have not received a high school diploma. Students who have a high school diploma will be given an enrichment program in related math and reading through college accredited courses. These skills will form a broad general base which can lead to further study and/or job advancement if the candidate so desires. Upon completion of the program, the student will be placed in job slots by the job developer, who will conduct a follow up on each candidate to study their progress. Students enrolled in this program receive $15 per week stipend to defray the cost of transportation and lunch.

Secretarial Science

A course of studies designed to prepare a student for assuming all the basic responsibilities of a private secretary. In addition, this program is designed to foster individual initiative in handling various business details.

Credit for Life Experiences

Many adult students have engaged in activities leading to the development of skills representing the behavioral objectives for certain college courses. As an example, an individual may have taught himself enough accounting to qualify for credit in Accounting. Another may have engaged in the varied functions of a small business operation to the extent that credit could be awarded. Still others may have had experiences as reporters for newspapers that would qualify them for credit in Journalism and English. Even more persons may have read widely and might, as a result of this intellectual activity, have gained sufficient insight and knowledge to qualify for credit in the Humanities or some aspect of the Social Sciences. Finally, the complex problem of surviving in the Ghetto may have given the individual more knowledge of the subdivisions of Sociology than could ever be gained by sitting in a classroom. These experiences could certainly merit college credit. Students should discuss the possibility of credit for Life Experiences with a member of the counseling staff or with the faculty adviser.

College Credit in Escrow

High school juniors and seniors seeking an intellectual challenge and a preview of college life will find the Malcolm X College Credit in Escrow program an exciting experience. High school juniors or seniors are eligible to apply if they receive the recommendation of their Principal. Classes will be conducted in local high schools and at Malcolm X College. Each class is limited to 25 students.

College credit will be held for the CCIE student until he enrolls at Malcolm X College or another college of his choice.

Directed Study for High School Credit

High school courses may be taken through independent directed study to complete a high school education or meet college entrance requirements. Outlines for specific courses are available upon request. These courses are available upon request and are accepted for full credit by institutions accredited by the North Central Association of Secondary Schools and Colleges.

General Education Development (High School GED Diploma)

Perhaps you never finished high school but now want to remove this obstacle to your vocational advancement. If so, contact the Department of Community Affairs and Continuing Education (telephone: 243-6475). Successful completion of the General Education Development (GED) test will qualify you for a diploma or equivalency certificate. Malcolm X College offers programs for individuals who do not have a high school diploma or for those who need a refresher course before entering a specific training program. A general background is offered in general math, grammar, literature, social studies and science. After a period of study, students can take the General Education Development (GED) examination and receive a high school diploma or equivalency certificate. The length of time needed to complete the program depends upon the individual student's rate of growth, progress, and interest.

The Independent Study Program

Correspondence study . . . study in home, study is independent, study is lifelong, study is continuing. All of these terms and others are used in connection with extension education which began about a century ago when large universities recognized that their responsibilities for the education of the people extended beyond the confines of the classroom walls. Malcolm X College subscribes to this principle.

A systematic program of studying at home offers an effective method of learning to attend classes at a given time and place. This plan is based on sound and tested principles of education. It makes it possible and practical for individuals to continue their education when other means are not available to them.

Independent Study Courses

HISTORY 111: History of the American People to 1865
HISTORY 112: History of the American People to 1865
HISTORY 114: The Afro-American in American History
HISTORY 222: English History from 1689
HISTORY 230: Ancient History
POLITICAL SCIENCE 201: National Government
POLITICAL SCIENCE 204: International Relations
PSYCHOLOGY 201: General Psychology
PSYCHOLOGY 215: Psychology of Personality
SOCIOLOGY 201: Introduction to the Study of Society
SOCIOLOGY 202: Sociology of Urban Life
SOCIOLOGY 206: Juvenile Delinquency

Parolee Assistance Program

The Department of Community Affairs and Continuing Education offers an intensive program to aid parolees (adult and juvenile) released from state and local correction institutions. Contact is initially made while the offender is in the institution and a program is developed which will assist his adjustment to the community. Through a cooperative program with private and public agencies, Malcolm X College is attacking the problem of recidivism, and is assisting parolees so that they will not return to the dehumanizing effects of the institution. College credit and non-credit courses are offered by staff members at various half-way houses. Parolees are encouraged to enroll at Malcolm X College. Counseling services are made available, and legal assistance is provided when needed.

Political Awareness Program

A Legislative Reference Office and a Voter's Information Program is available through the Department of Community Affairs and Continuing Education. Close liaison is maintained with national, state and local legislative bodies. Information pertaining to legislation which affects the general and educational community is followed. Participants in this program appear at hearings and engage in other activities to assure proper representation of the community.

A Voter's Education Program is an ongoing activity of this office.

Prison Annex

Malcolm X College provides relevant and meaningful college level courses to inmates of various state correction institutions. Malcolm X offers a valuable opportunity to persons who have been incarcerated to develop a bridge between the prison and the community through study. Courses offered are taught through a visiting faculty program, correspondence courses, telephone lecture-discussion programs, or a combination of methods. Follow-up and continued association with Malcolm X College is available, if desired by the student. College credit earned through the Prison Annex is entered on a college transcript to be held in escrow until the student enrolls at Malcolm X or asks that it be sent to another college.

Malcolm X College Speaker's Bureau

The Malcolm X College Speaker's Bureau provides a service to community social and political organizations. Members of the administration, faculty and student body are available to these organizations on various relevant and meaningful topics such as (not restricted to) the following:

The Philosophy of Malcolm X College
The Programs of Malcolm X College
Afro–American History
Afro–American Art, Drama or Music
The Urban Crisis
Urban Education and Minority Groups

Organizations requesting further information should write to: Malcolm X College Speakers' Bureau, 1900 West Van Buren, Chicago, Ill. 60612.

Social Service
The Malcolm X College Urban Studies Institute offers courses usually considered desirable at the undergraduate level for students who plan to continue their studies in Social Service Administration. It is suggested that such students inquire about specific requirements from the Four Year College of their choice. Although students may plan a limited career in this field with only a Bachelor's Degree, in order to work at the professional level a minimum of a Master's Degree is necessary.

The purpose of the Pre-Social Service courses are:

1. To provide an understanding of the programs established for man's social betterment.

2. To provide a general preparation for pre-professional employment in the social field.

Appropriate majors for students interested in Social Service Administration are Sociology and Psychology.

Street Academy
Malcolm X College recognizes its obligation to assist in educating those members of the community who have been unable to continue their education in the city's public schools. The Street Academy recruits those members of the community of all ages who desire to complete their education in order to remove obstacles which have been erected to prevent their advancement in our society. Services to the community include counseling (educational and employment), tutorial work in basic educational skills (reading, writing, and arithmetic), GED review, technical and vocational training, etc. The Street Academy accepts the principle that educational methods must be adapted to the needs of the community. In accordance with this principle, Malcolm X College extends its educational services to men and women of all ages whom circumstances prevented from getting a proper education. The Malcolm X Street Academy brings the school to the student through the establishment of store-front classrooms, educational outposts, and making day care services available for mothers and others responsible for child care to attend school.

Core Curriculum in Liberation

The following courses carry no credit toward the AA Degree, but are required for receipt of the certificate showing completion of a curriculum in "Liberation and Freedom."

Afro–American Culture Series
Black Achievement
Black Education Seminar
Black Health
Black Humanism Series
Black Soul Search
Black Women's Liberation Series
Karate for Self-Defense
Latin–American Series
Liberation Series
Marksmanship
Political Action Series
Project Diploma
Seminar in Revolution and Freedom
War on Illiteracy
Youth

Week End College

It is possible for you to enroll for college credit courses offered near where you live at Malcolm X on Saturdays and Sundays. The College has scheduled a large number of classes between 9:00 and 4:00 P.M. on Saturdays and Sundays. The Week-End College will provide an opportunity to learn for members of the community who work and whose family responsibilities make attendance at the week day or evening classes impossible.

The Black Studies Institute

Established in June, 1969, the Black Studies Institute provides a variety of academic and cultural activities. The Institute will create a two-year program leading to the Associate of Arts Degree in Black Studies, in which the student may concentrate in Afro–American Studies and African Studies. The classroom activities of the Black Studies curriculum will be reinforced by the creation of the Black Studies Library and Research Center, providing access for the student seriously committed to a major in Black Studies, to books, records, tapes and films related to the Black Experience. Moreover, The Black Forum will present throughout the academic year, lectures by outstanding Black scholars in the arts and sciences and cultural activities such as commemorative programs for deceased Black historical figures and an annual Black Arts Festival will be presented.

The Community Extension Program, in conjunction with the Division of Community Relations will present Adult Education courses in Black Thought and Culture and assume supportive roles in the civic activities of the Community.

BIBLIOGRAPHY

Allen, Patricia R. and Weathersby, Rita E. *Minorities in the curriculum: What's Happening Where; an informal survey of programs and resources in Massachusetts.* Paper prepared for a conference, "Minorities and the Curriculum" (Natick, Mass., May 10, 1969). 1969. 69p.

America, Richard F., Jr., "The Case of the Racist Researchers." *Black World*, May, 1970.

Axem, Richard; Devern, Pentony; Smith, Robert. *By Any Means Necessary: The Revolutionary Struggle at San Francisco State.* San Francisco: Jossey-Bass, 1970.

Baird, Bernard. "Black Studies Behind New Campus Battlecry," *The New York Post*, p. 25, March 15, 1969.

Banathy, Be la H. *Instructional Systems.* Palo Alto: Fearon Publishers, 1968.

Barker, Horace, *The Federal Retreat in School Desegregation. Special Report.* Atlanta: Southern Regional Council, 1969. 76 p.

Bendiver, Robert. *The Politics of Schools.* New York: Harper and Row, 1969.

Bennett, Lerone, Jr. "Liberation." In special edition of *Ebony Magazine—Which Way, Black America.* Chicago: Johnson Publications, August, 1970.

Billingsley, Andrew, *et al.* "Ethnic Studies at Berkeley." *California Monthly*, 8:12–20, June-July 1970.

Birch, Herbert G. *Health and the Education of Socially Disadvantaged Children.* Atlanta: Southern Regional Council.

Birenbaum, William. *Overlive.* New York: Delta, 1969.

Black Lines, A Journal of Black Studies.

Bloom, Benjamin S., "Learning for Mastery." *UCLA Evaluation Comment.* Vol. I, No. 2, May, 1968.

Bonjean, Charles M. (ed.). "Black American." *Social Science Quarterly*, 1968, 49 (3) pp. 427–741.

Bornholdt, Laura. "Black Studies: Perspective, 1970." *Danforth News and Notes*, 5:1, March, 1970.

Boyd, William L. and Campbell, Ronald F. "Organizational Alternatives for Secondary Schools." *The North Central Association Quarterly*, The North Central Association of Colleges and Secondary Schools, Vol. XLV, No. 2, Fall 1970.

Brawer, Florence B. and Cohen, Arthur M. "Focus on Learning: Preparing Teachers for the Two-Year College." *USCLA Graduate School of Education, Occasional Report*, Number 11, (March 1968), p. 24.

Brietman, George, Malcolm X. *By Any Means Necessary.* New York: Pathfinder Press, 1970.

Brown, Dee. *Bury My Heart at Wounded Knee.* New York: Holt, Rinehart & Winston, 1971.

Browne, Robert S. "The Challenge of Black Student Organizations," *Freedomways*, pp. 325–333, Fall, 1968.

Brudney, David. "Black Power and the Campus," *National Review*, October 8, 1968.

Bunzel, John H. "Black Studies at San Francisco State," *The Public Interest*, no. 13, pp. 324–325, Fall, 1968.

Burrows, David and Lopides, Frederick R. *Racism.* New York: Thomas Y. Crowell Company, 1970.

Carmichael, Stokely and Hamilton, Charles. *Black Power: The Politics of Liberation in America.* New York: A Vintage Book, 1967.

Carmichael, Stokely. "Pan-Africanism: Land and Power." *The Black Scholar.*

Carnegie Commission on Higher Education. *Less Time, More Options: Education Beyond the High School.* New York: McGraw-Hill Book Co., 1970.

Change. September-October 1969. p. 6.

Cobbs, Price M., and Grier, Williams H. *Black Rage.* New York: Basic Books, 1968.

Coleman, James S. "Equal Schools or Equal Students?" *Policy Issues in Urban Education,* Smilery, Marjorie B. and Miller, Harry L., ed New York: The Free Press, 1968.

Coleman, James S. "Equality of Educational Opportunity." U.S. Dept. of Health, Education and Welfare, Office of Education, Washington, D.C., Superintendent of Documents, Government Printing Office, 1966.

Conant, James B. *Slums and Suburbs.* New York: The New American Library, McGraw-Hill Book Co., 1961.

"The Communiversity: An Alternative Independent System." *Negro Digest,* 19 (5) March 1970, pp. 25–29, 72–74.

Coombs, Phillip H. *The World Educational Crisis.* New York: Oxford University Press, 1969.

Crow, John E. *Discrimination, Poverty, and the Negro: Arizona in the National Context.* Tucson: The University of Arizona Press, 1968.

Dennison, George. *The Lives of Children.* New York: Random House, 1969.

Dentler, Robert, Mackler, Bernard, and Warshauer, Mary Ellen. *The Urban R's: Race Relations as the Problem in Urban Education.* New York: Frederick A. Praeger, 1967.

Dickinson, Donald C. *A Bio-bibliography of Langston Hughes, 1902–1967.* Second edition. Hamden, Connecticut: Archon Books, 1972.

DuBois, W. E. B. *Africa in Battle Against Colonialism, Racialism, Imperialism.* Chicago: Afro–American Books, 1969, 1964.

DuBois, W. E. B. *Autobiography of W. E. B. DuBois.* New York: International Publishers, 1968.

DuBois, W. E. B. "Can the Negro Expect Freedom by 1965?" *Negro Digest,* April, 1947.

DuBois, W. E. B. "Careers Open to College-Bred Negroes," in *Two Addresses.* Nashville: Fisk University, 1898.

DuBois, W. E. B. "The Development of a People." *International Journal of Ethics,* April, 1904.

DuBois, W. E. B. "Education in Africa." *Crisis,* June, 1926.

DuBois, W. E. B. "Education and Work." *Howard University Bulletin,* Jan. 1931. (*Journal of Negro Education,* April 1932.)

DuBois, W. E. B. "Education, 1928." *Crisis*, August, 1928.

DuBois, W. E. B. "The Freedom to Learn." *Midwest Journal*, Winter, 1949.

DuBois, W. E. B. "The Future of the Negro Race in America." *East and the West*, Vol. II, No. 5, 1904.

DuBois, W. E. B. *Mortality Among Negroes in Cities*. Atlanta: Atlanta University Press, Atlanta Study No. 1, 1896.

DuBois, W. E. B. "Negro in College." *Nation*, March, 1926.

DuBois, W. E. B. "The Negro Race in the United States of America." in G. Spiller (ed.), *Papers on Interracial Problems*. London: P. S. King & Son; Boston: World's Peace Foundation, 1911, pp. 348–364.

DuBois, W. E. B. "The Negro Scientist." *American Scholar*, July, 1939.

DuBois, W. E. B. "On Being Ashamed of Oneself. An Essay on Race Pride." *Crisis*, September, 1933.

DuBois, W. E. B. "Prospect of a World Without Race Conflict." *American Journal of Sociology*, March, 1944.

DuBois, W. E. B. "The Immortal Child-Background on Crises in Education." (pamphlet). Chicago: Afro–American Books, 1964.

DuBois, W. E. B. *The Souls of Black Folk*. New York: New American Library, June, 1969.

DuBois, W. E. B. "The Talented Tenth." in Booker T. Washington (ed.), *The Negro Problem*. New York: James Pott Co., 1903.

Dunbar, Ernest. "The Black Studies Thing." *New York Times* (Magazine section), April 16, 1969.

Dye, Thomas R. "Urban School Segregation: A Comparative Analysis." *Urban Affairs Quarterly*, 1968, 4 (2), pp. 141–165.

Fanon, Frantz. *Black Skin: White Masks*. New York: Grove Press, Inc., 1967.

Fanon, Frantz. *The Wretched of the Earth: A Negro Psychiatrist's Study of the Problems of Racism and Colonialism in the World Today*. New York: Grove Press, Inc., 1966.

Fantini, Mario D. and Weinstein, Gerald. *The disadvantaged: challenge to education*. New York: Harper & Row, 1968.

Fischer, John H. "Race and Reconciliation: The Role of the School." *Daedalus*, Winter, 1966.

Franklin, John Hope. "Rediscovering Black America: A Historical Roundup." *New York Times Book Review*, September 8, 1968.

Franklin, John Hope. "The Two Worlds of Race: A Historical View." *Daedalus*, Vol. 94, No. 4, Fall, 1965.

Gardner, John W. *The Recovery of Confidence*. New York: W. W. Norton, Inc., 1970.

Gibson, John S. *The development of instructional materials and teaching strategies on race and culture in American Life. Final report—volume I, II first part, II second part, III*. Medford, Mass.: Lincoln Filene Center for Citizenship and Public Affairs, Tufts University, 1968.

Gilbert, Ben W. and Staff of *The Washington Post*. *Ten Blocks from the White House: Anatomy of the Washington Riots of 1968*. New York: Frederick A. Praeger, 1968.

Glosser, William. *Schools Without Failure*. New York: Harper and Row, 1969.

Goldberg, Gertrude S. *New Nonprofessionals in the Human Services: An Overview*. Atlanta: Southern Regional Council.

Goldberg, Gertrude S. *Job and Career Development for the Poor— The Human Services*. Atlanta: Southern Regional Council.

Goodman, Paul. "The present moment in education." *The New York Review of Books*, 12(7):14–24, April 10, 1969.

Gordon, Edmund W. and Joblonsky, Adelaide. *Compensatory Education in the Equalization of Educational Opportunity*. Atlanta: Southern Regional Council.

Greeley, Andrew M. "The New Urban Studies," *Educational Record*. Beverly Hills, California: Sage Publications, Summer, 1970.

Green, Robert (ed.). *Racial Crisis In American Education*. Chicago: Follett Educational Corp., 1969.

Grundstein, Nathan D. "The Public School: System Change and Management Science." *Education and Urban Society*. Beverly Hills, California: Sage Publications, November, 1970.

Hamilton, Charles, "Race and Education: A Search for Legitimacy." *Harvard Educational Review*, 1968, 38 (4), pp. 669–684.

Hamilton, Charles V. "Relevance of Black Studies?" In G. K. Smith (ed.), *Agony and Promises. Current Issues in Higher Education*. San Francisco: Jossey-Bass, 1969.

Harding, Vincent. "Black Students and the Impossible Revolution." *Journal of Black Studies*, 1:75–100, September 1970.

Harding, Vincent. "Toward the Black University." *Ebony*, 25:158, August 1970.

Hart, Leslie A. *The Classroom Disaster*. New York: Teachers College
Press, Columbia University, 1969.

Hauser, Philip M. and Hodge, Patricia L. *The Challenge of America's Metropolitan Population Outlook*. New York, 1960.

Heermance, J. Noel. *William Wells Brown and Clotelle: A Por-
trait of the Artist in the First Negro Novel*. Hamden, Connecticut:
Archon Books, 1969.

Heiss, Ann M. *Challenges to Graduate Schools*. San Francisco:
Jossey-Bass, 1970.

Herrscher, Barton R. and Roueche, John E. (eds.). "A Learning Oriented System of Instruction." *Junior College Instruction*, Selected
Academic Readings, 1970.

Herskovits, Melville. *The New World Negro: Selected Papers in
Afro–American Studies*. Bloomington: Indiana U. Press, 1966.

Hester, Julius. *Look Out, Whitey! Black Power's Gon' Get You
Mama!* New York: Grove Press, 1968.

Hill, Roscoe and Feeley, Malcolm (eds.). *Affirmative School Integration: Efforts to Overcome De Facto Segregation in Urban Schools*.
Beverly Hills: Sage Publications, 1968.

Howie, Donald, "The Origins of Racism: A Problem in African–
American History." *Negro Digest*, 19 (4) February 1970, pp. 39–47.

Hurst, Charles G., Jr. "Malcolm X: A Community College with a
New Perspective," *Black Digest*, Johnson Publications, March,
1970.

Huxley, Aldous. *Education on Nonverbal Level in Revolution in
Teaching: New Theory, Technology and Curricula*. New York:
Bantam Books, 1964.

*Integrated School Books: A Descriptive Bibliography of 399 Pre-
School and Elementary School Texts and Story Books*. New York:
NAACP Education Department, 1967.

Jacobson, Barbara. "Education: Social Factory or Social Process."
American Behavioral Scientist. Beverly Hills, California: Sage Publications, November, 1970.

Katzman, Martin T. "Discrimination, Subculture, and the Economic
Performance of Negro, Puerto Ricans, and Mexican–Americans."
American Journal of Economics and Sociology, 1968, 27 (4), pp.
371–375.

Kent, James K. "The Coleman Report: Opening Pandora's Box,"

The Politics of Urban Education, Gittell, Marilyn and Hevesi, Alan C., eds. New York: Frederick A. Praeger, 1969.

Kirp, David L. "Race, Class, and the Limits of Schooling," *Urban Review.* 4 (3) May, 1970, pp. 10–13.

Kirp, David L. "The Poor, the School, and Equal Protection." *Harvard Educational Review,* 1968, 38 (4) pp. 635–668.

Kirschner, Joseph. "Education as Technology: Implications from the History of an Idea." *The Record,* 1968, 70 (2), pp. 121–126.

Knight, Etheridge. *Black Voices From Prison.* New York: Pathfinder Press, Inc., 1970.

Knoell, Dorothy M. *Black Student Potential.* Washington, D.C.: American Association of Junior Colleges, 1970.

Kochman, Thomas. "Rapping in the Black Ghetto." *Transaction,* February, 1969.

Kohl, Herbert R. *The Open Classroom.* New York: Random House, Inc., 1969.

Lawlessness and Disorder: Fourteen Years of Failure in Southern School Desegregation. Special Report, 1968. 64 pp. Atlanta: Southern Regional Council, 1968.

Leococh, Eleonor Burke. *Teaching and Learning in City Schools.* New York: Basic Books, Inc., 1969.

Lessinger, Leon. *Every Kid A Winner: Accountability in Education.* New York: Simon and Schuster, 1970.

Lloyd, P. C. *African in Social Change: West African Societies in Transition.* New York: Frederick A. Praeger, 1968.

Lowe, Keith. "Toward a Black University," *Liberator,* September, 1968.

Lowi, Theodore J., "Apartheid U.S.A.: Federally Assisted Urban Redevelopment—A Blueprint for Segregation," *Transaction,* 7 (4) 1970 pp. 32–39.

Mager, Robert. *Developing Attitudes Toward Learning.* Palo Alto: Fearon Publishers, 1968.

Memm, Albert. *The Colonizer and the Colonized.* Boston: Beacon Press, 1965.

Moynihan, Daniel P. "Policy vs. Program in the '70's, *Public Interest,* 20 Summer, 1970, pp. 90–100.

Myrdal, Gunnar. *An American Dilemma: The Negro Problem and Democracy.* New York: Harper and Row, 1963.

Nyerere, Julius K. "Education for Self-Reliance." Washington, D.C.: *Information Bulletin, Embassy of the Republic of Tanzania,* March, 1967.

Ornstein, Allan C. "School Desegregation and Integration." *Illinois Schools Journal,* Chicago State College, Chicago, Fall, 1970.

Palmer, L. E. "Blacks Fear Plan for Mental Health Data Bank." *Chicago Daily News,* Saturday-Sunday, April 25-26, p. 10.

Pettigrew, Thomas F. "Complexity and Change in American Racial Patterns: A Social Psychological View." *Daedalus,* Fall, 1965.

Pettigrew, Thomas F. "Race and Equal Educational Opportunity," *Harvard Educational Review,* 38, pp. 67–76, 1968.

Rosovsky, Henry. *Report of the Faculty Committee on African and Afro–American Studies.* Cambridge: Harvard University Press, 1969.

Rousseve, R. "Teachers of Culturally Disadvantaged American Youth." *Journal of Negro Education,* 1963, 32, pp. 114–121.

S.A.S. Presents Plan for Autonomous Black Institute," *Columbia Spectator,* pp. 1, 2, February 28, 1969.

Saunders, Charles. "Assessing Race Relations Research," *Black Scholar,* 1 (5) March, 1970, pp. 17–25.

Segal, Julius, (ed.). *The Mental Health of the Child,* National Institute of Mental Health, Washington, D.C.

Silberman, Charles E. *Crisis in the Classroom.* New York: Random House, 1970.

Stodolsky, Susan S. and Lesser, Gerald S. *Learning Patterns in the Disadvantaged.* Atlanta: Southern Regional Council.

Torrey, Jane W. "Illiteracy in the Ghetto," *Harvard Educational Review,* Vol. 40, No. 2, May, 1970.

Tucker, Sterling. *Black Reflections on White Power.* Grand Rapids, Mich.: Wm. B. Eerdman Publishing Company, 1969.

Wade, Georgett. "Opening Fall Enrollment in Higher Education, 1969." *U.S. Office of Education,* Washington, D.C. 1970.

Walton, Sidney F., Jr., (ed.). *The Black Curriculum: Developing a Program in Afro–American Studies.* Oakland, California: Black Liberation Publishers, 1968. [Available through Black Liberation Publishers, 740-60th Street, Oakland, California 94609. Includes a discussion of the rationale for Afro–American studies and a selected bibliography for classroom use.]

Ware, Claude. "The Dynamics of the Ethnic Studies Program." Los Angeles City College, 1969 (mimeo).

Webster, Staten W., (ed.). *Knowing the Disadvantaged.* San Francisco: Chandler Publishing Co., 1970.

Weinberg, Meyer. "The Education of the Minority Child (A Comprehensive Bibliography)." Integrated Educated Associates, Chicago, 1970.

Weinberg, Meyer. *Integrated Education.* Beverly Hills, California: The Glencoe Press, 1968.

White, Doris. *Multi-ethnic books for Head Start Children, part I: black and integrated literature; part II: other minority group literature.* Urbana, Illinois: National Laboratory on Early Childhood Education, 1969.

Wilcox, Preston. "Black Power Conference Reports." New York: Action Library, Afram Associates, 1970.

Wilcox, Preston. "Black Studies as an American Discipline," *Negro Digest*, 19 (5) March 1970, pp. 75–87.

Williams, Frederick. "Implications of Recent Research in Social Dialects for Speech Communication Education." SAA Summer Conference, 1970.

Williams, Robert L. "Testing and Dehumanizing Black Children," (unpublished paper), 1970.

Williams, Robert L. "Watch Out! Testin' is Harmful to Black Children." (unpublished paper), 1970.

Woodson, Carter G. *The Mis-education of the Negro.* Washington, D.C.: The Associated Publishers, 1933.

"Malcolm X on Afro–American History," *International Socialist Review*, p. 4, March-April, 1964.

Periodicals

Afro–American, 628 W. Utah Street, Baltimore, Maryland 21233

American Historical Review, 400 "A" Street, S.E., Washington, D.C. 20003

Bayviewee, 2049 Ashby Ave., Berkeley, California 94703

Black Digest, 1820 S. Michigan Avenue, Chicago, Illinois 60616

Black Academy Review, 3296 Main St., Buffalo, N.Y. 14214

Black Expressions, 7512 S. Cottage Grove, Chicago, Illinois 60619

Black Lines, P.O. Box 7195, Oakland Station, Pittsburgh, Pennsylvania 15213

Black News, 10 Claver Pl., Brooklyn, N.Y. 11238

Black Scholar, P.O. Box 908, Sausalito, California 94965

Black Times, 1260 Brighton, 305, Albany, California 94706

Black World, 1820 South Michigan Avenue, Chicago, Illinois 60616

Chicago Defender, 2400 S. Michigan Avenue, Chicago, Illinois 60616

Crisis, (NAACP) 40th Street, New York, N.Y. 10027

Defender (U.S.), 1400 French St., Wilmington, Delaware 19801

Ebony Magazine, 1820 S. Michigan Avenue, Chicago, Illinois 60616

Essence, 102 E. 30th Street, New York, N.Y. 10016

Focus in Black, 5877 Grand Central Sta., New York, N.Y. 10017

Freedomways, 799 Broadway, New York, N.Y. 10013

Harvard Journal of Afro–American Affairs, 20 Sacramento St., Cambridge, Massachusetts 02138

Integrated Education, 343 S. Dearborn Street, Chicago, Illinois 60604

Jet, 1820 South Michigan Avenue, Chicago, Illinois 60616

Journal of Black Studies, 275 S. Beverly Dr., Beverly Hills, California 90212

Journal of Negro Education, Bureau of Educational Research, Howard University, Washington, D.C. 20001

Journal of Negro History, 1401 Fourteenth St., N.W., Washington, D.C. 20005   ,

Liberator, 244 E. 46th Street, New York, N.Y. 10007

Negro Educational Review, P.O. Box 741, Nashville, Tennessee 37202

Negro History Bulletin, 1538 Ninth Street, N.W., Washington, D.C. 20001

N. Y. Courier, 61 W. 130 St., New York, N.Y. 10027

Soul Illustrated, 271 Melrose Avenue, Los Angeles, California 90046

Tuesday Publications, 180 North Michigan Avenue, Chicago, Illinois 60616

INDEX